BEAUTIFUL UNITY

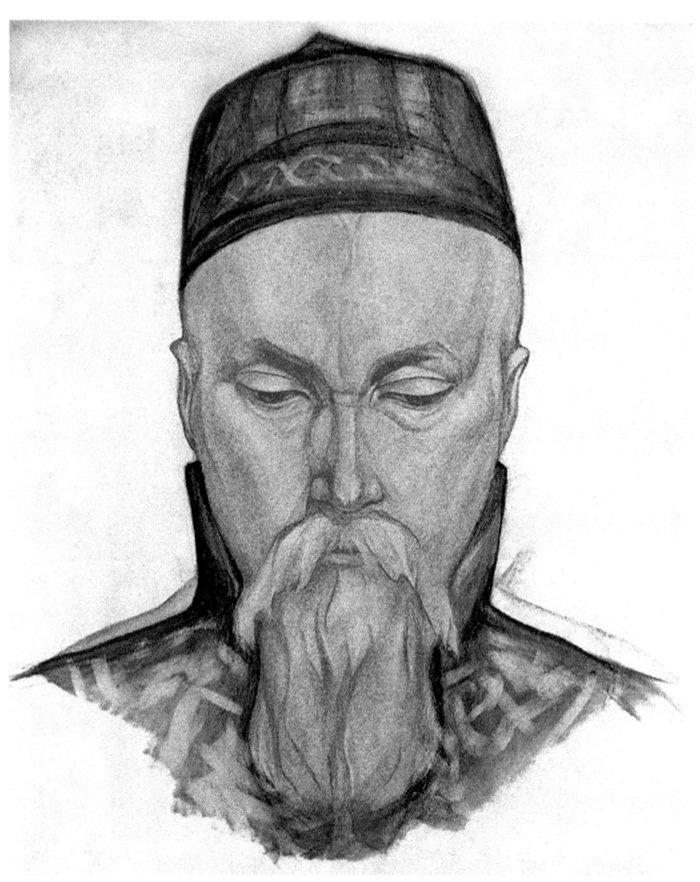

Portrait of Nicholas Roerich by Svetoslav Roerich

BEAUTIFUL UNITY

NICHOLAS ROERICH

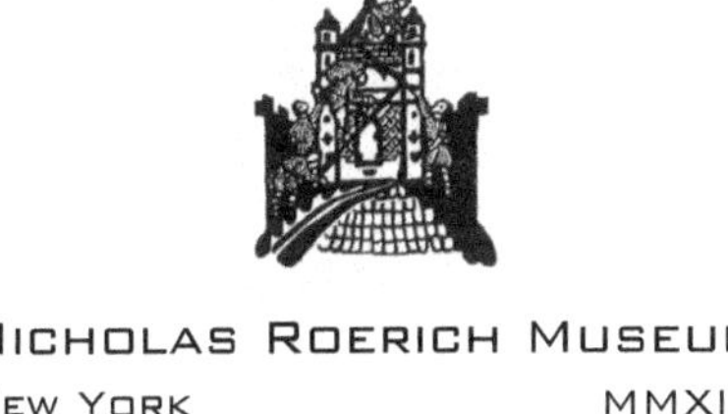

NICHOLAS ROERICH MUSEUM

NEW YORK   MMXIX

Nicholas Roerich Museum
319 West 107th Street
New York NY 10025
www.roerich.org

Cover illustration: Nicholas Roerich. *Star of the Morning.* 1932.

FOREWORD TO THE FIRST EDITION

NICHOLAS ROERICH has a place all his own in the world of Art. His pen too has carved out a niche for itself in the world of letters. The brush has a wider appeal no doubt, but the pen has a distinct function of its own; and in the hands of Nicholas Roerich it has for long exerted an influence which is at once elevating and instructive. A call to Beauty implies in its essentials an appreciation of the Vision which the Artist would fain share with the world at large. That the Artist's vision even when expressed in rhetoric can be quite as sincere as when it finds expression through line and color and form is amply evidenced by what is set forth in this volume of essays. I am happy to find that in the following pages my friend Nicholas Roerich has voiced what fundamentally every sensitive mind feels about the values of Art including what is perhaps the greatest of all Arts—the Art of Living. In this he has indeed spoken for all Artists. I am sure the book will receive the recognition which is its due.

ABANINDRANATH TAGORE
Santiniketan, March 15, 1946

CONTENTS

BEAUTIFUL UNITY

Art will unify all humanity. Art is one—indivisible. Art has its many branches, yet all are one. Art is the manifestation of the coming synthesis; art is for all. Everyone will enjoy true art. The gates of the 'sacred source' must be wide open for everybody, and the light of art will influence numerous hearts with a new love. At first this feeling will be unconscious, but after all it will purify human consciousness, and how many young hearts are searching for something real and beautiful! So give it to them. Bring art to the people—where it belongs. We should have not only museums, theaters, universities, public libraries, railway stations and hospitals, but even prisons decorated and beautified. Then we shall have no more prisons.

Humanity is facing the coming events of cosmic greatness. Humanity already realizes that all occurrences are not accidental. The time for the construction of future culture is at hand. Before our eyes the reassessment of values is being witnessed. Amidst ruins of valueless banknotes, mankind has found the real value of the world's significance. The values of great art and knowledge are victoriously traversing all storms of earthly commotions. Even the 'earthly' people already understand the vital importance of a beauty that is alive. And when we proclaim: labor, beauty and action, we know verily that we pronounce the formula of the international language. And this formula, which now belongs to the museum and stage must enter into everyday life. The sign of beauty and action will open all gates. Beneath the sign of beauty we walk joyfully. With beauty and labor we conquer. In beauty we are united. And now we affirm these words—not on the snowy heights, but amidst the turmoil of the city. And realizing the path of true reality, we greet the future with a happy smile.

NICHOLAS ROERICH

BEAUTIFUL UNITY

COLOR, sound and fragrance are cornerstones of great synthesis. From time immemorial people have felt the great inner meaning of these expressions of the human soul. Quite recently people have begun again to remember how close are color and sound and that the three are the basic remedies against human diseases. Thus he who thinks about the conception of color does not at all associate it with paint as such, but he has in mind one of the greatest concepts of our existence.

The color value of a painting, indeed, does not mean the mere value of paint but of its harmonic correlation, as the French say "Valeur." What does such a correlation mean? Again we must say that for him who is ignorant of the concepts of synthesis and symphony, such correlation will be an empty word.

Let us not dwell here on the deep significance of art for human life—this axiom should be clear to everyone. But nowadays we must especially stress the meaning of synthesis and the symphony of life. Synthesis will be understood by everyone to whom the concept of Culture is close. If human thinking were to remain but on the level of elementary civilization, then it would be too early to mention sacred synthesis, but where the human spirit has traveled towards Culture—that is to say, the Cult of Light—there one may already find co-operation and understanding based on synthesis.

If civilization has not saved humanity from disunity and mutual hatred, then Culture has opened the beneficial gates of synthesis, behind which we can find true co-operation.

The artists do not rest on primitive considerations of paint, but the very understanding of the sonority of color leads them to such beautiful gardens from where superb vistas of the glorious future may be seen. When we speak of synthesis and of the symphony of life, we shall not avoid powerful and enthusiastic expressions. All these domains of synthesis and symphony are uplifting and lead to the summits. Often the human eye can hardly stand the radiance of snowy peaks and it is not for the human eye to judge the splendor of these summits. But we have not been called into this world to criticize, but to labor, to admire and to follow these leading summits in continuous creation.

Create, Create and Create! Create in daytime, create at night; for creation in thought is as essential as our physical expression. In this creativeness you shall overcome the most hideous habits of vulgarity, triviality and quarrelling. People sometimes think that creators are very selfish and conceited. But these ugly properties belong to the domain of darkness. When a person "climbs" to the Light, then such an abhorrent husk drops off by itself and man becomes enlightened. His "I," is changed into the concept of "We."

On the same path towards the summits, man will understand the true meaning of Guruship. From the depth of darkness one can hear disgusting cries at present: "Down with culture," "Down with heroes," "Down with teachers." It is a shame on humanity, but one witnesses such outcries of crass ignorance even nowadays. But he who thinks of such a refined conception as color and sound, culture and harmony, he will understand the infinite Hierarchy of Beauty and Knowledge, and having ascended the majestic stairs of achievement, he will also lead the pilgrims of life who are following behind.

It is splendid that you are young—some in age, and some in spirit. Around creativeness there must be this perpetual feeling of youth which gives incessant striving towards heroism. Countries measure their glory not by captains of industry, but by artists and scientists. Such a requirement of history places upon us the duty of incessant perfectionment. He who never ceases to ascend never becomes old.

I send you my heartiest greetings on this path towards the radiant summits and I trust that you, forgetting all petty divisions and small human moods, will progress in continuous creation, cherishing the glorious traditions of your great Motherland, India!

Nalini Kanta Gupta writes in the *Triveni*, in his article on the "Beautiful in the Upanishads":

"Art at its highest tends to become also the simplest and the most unconventional; and it is then the highest art, precisely because it does not aim at being artistic. The aesthetic motive is totally absent in the Upanishads: the sense of beauty is there, but it is attendant upon and involved in a deeper strand of consciousness."

Verily Art at its highest does not tolerate any conventionality, nor violence. In the very foundations of Be-ness lives the concept of Beauty in all its power.

We, as builders, do not deny, nor reject.

> "In Beauty we are united!
> Through Beauty we pray!
> With Beauty we conquer!"

RENAISSANCE

IN India a glorious Renaissance of Art is approaching. New Schools will be opened. Exhibition Halls will be built. Museums will grow. Besides State Museums, many private collections will be founded, not only of ancient art, but of modern art as well. It would be instructive to have the annals of the names of the new private collectors. In the history of Indian Art, the names of these ardent lovers of Beauty will be given a place of great honor.

The illustrious patron of art, the Duke Moro once told Leonardo da Vinci: "He who shall venerate the name of Leonardo shall also remember Moro."

From ancient times collecting has been a sign of stability and introspection. It is very instructive to survey the various means and ways of collecting and of studying art from our days down to the heart of antiquity. Again, as in all the spirals of growth, we see almost complete circles; yet at times, an almost elusive heightening of consciousness forms another step which is reflected in many pages of the history of art. We see how specialization and synthesis alternate. Collecting formed by the inner consciousness of the collector and united by one general idea is replaced by a classification, almost pharmaceutical, sometimes completely destroying the fire of new discoveries with its pedantry. Not so long ago, the combining of Gothic primitives with modern aspirations would have been considered a proof of dilettantism. It would have been regarded as completely taboo to simply have a collection of beautiful medals and coins. Pedantry was wont to confine its scope of vision to a certain epoch, limiting it to the objects of a certain type and character. Thus icons and primitives glowing with color were turned into iconography in which the descriptive part obliterated the true and artistic meaning.

Thus, not very long ago, the history of art was taught as a collection of anecdotes of painters' lives, while the exposition of sculptures and the technique of painting were reduced to a summary of proportions and to the mechanics of construction, diverting and distracting attention from the essence of creative work. Peculiar textbooks began to appear in which one would come across such chapters, for example, as: "How to paint a donkey, in connection with which gray paint—which does not exist—was recommended. I remember that my attention was caught, while on a boat, by the typical argument between a mother and her little girl in which the mother earnestly asserted that the mountain in the distance was black, while the child affirmed candidly that it was blue. It seems to me that the mother's eyes must have been dimmed by some textbook she was studying about the way to paint donkeys."

What a joy it is for children, when from their tenderest age they see objects of true art and serious books in their homes! Of course, it is necessary that these artistic objects continue to "live" and do not find themselves in the pitiful situation of remaining upside down, sometimes for an entire decade, which means that the soul of the collector has long departed for the cemetery and that his heirs have for some reason become morally blind.

During the most recent years, we have had occasion to rejoice many times over the synthetic system of collecting which has again come into existence. Not afraid of being called eccentrics or dilettantes, the sensitive collectors have begun to group their treasuries of various objects according to an inner meaning. Thus, the most modern pictures could be combined with those masters who, in their time, burned with the unquenchable fire of bringing new methods to their creative work.

In the newest collections one sees such giant pathfinders as El Greco, Giorgione, Peter Breugel and all the noble galaxy of those who were not afraid to be considered the seekers and innovators of their epochs.

And how convincing among modern paintings are the forms of Roman art and the collaborators Giotto and Cimabue, and the icons of Novgorod and ancient Chinese artists.

As all conventionalities of division and demarcation vanish, the combined creative and spiritual findings shine before you like beacon lights outside the conventional boundaries of the nations. If circumstances do not permit bringing originals into homes, then sketches and even well-reproduced copies could permit one to entertain happy dreams about the future.

I have had occasion to write the stirring story of those collectors who began their activities when still at school. Probably many painters have had experiences like mine of having little boys, who, coming to one of my exhibitions, would bashfully hand me a dollar asking to be given a sketch in return.

Another still more moving case was when public school pupils raised a collection in order to purchase a painting. That meant that ardor was stirring and taking shape within them, and that they wanted to transmute meaningless words into facts, into conscious action. Without such an imperative impulse to action, how many light-winged, thought-butterflies singe themselves in their flutterings!

In various countries, we can help with experience and advice concerning the question of how to begin collecting. One of our immediate obligations is to open the door to those who knock timidly. And not only to open the door, but also to explain that they should knock with a firm hand without entertaining the prejudices that the use of art is a privilege available only to the rich. No, first of all it is the privilege of bright and courageous spirits who long to beautify their existence and who have decided—instead of choosing the deadly hazards of gambling—to strengthen themselves by the manifestations of the spirit of man which, like an infinite dynamo, breathes life into everything made by it. Great joys are to be found at this feast of creative impulses. And many dark places in life can be so easily brightened by the brilliant rays of admiration. It is our sacred duty to help in this.

We are speaking about collecting. Someone smiles wryly: Is it timely? Is it timely to speak of artistic values when even the richest countries are horror-stricken by the general crisis? Let us answer him firmly and with the realization of the import of our words—Yes, it is timely.

According to the latest reports, in spite of the tremendous business depression in America, the prices for art objects have not suffered any depreciation and this does not surprise us in the least; on the contrary, we consider this to be a characteristic sign of the existence of the crisis.

We have seen that during the most acute crisis in Russia, Austria and Germany, the prices of art objects did not fluctuate noticeably. In some cases the art objects were instrumental in bringing an entire state out of financial difficulties. We preserve this irrefutable fact as a proof of the true value of the spirit of man. When all our conditional values are shaken, the consciousness of man instinctively turns to that which, amidst the ephemeral, proves to be relatively the most valuable.

And the spiritual, creative values which have been neglected during the triumph of the stomach again become a shelter of refuge. Therefore it is always timely to speak of the growth of spiritual creative power and to lay stress upon collecting and preserving. This is especially needed when evolution passes through difficult moments when the solution of the current accumulated problems is not known. To solve them, however, is possible only in spirit and in beauty.

In my address on the significance of art, I gave formulae which have become the motto of the International Art Centre. I said: "Humanity is facing events of cosmic greatness. Humanity already realizes that all occurrences are not accidental. The time for the construction of a future culture is at hand. The reassessment of values has taken place before our very eyes. Amidst heaps of what is valueless, current humanity has found a treasure of world significance. The values of great art march victoriously through the storms of earthly commotions. Even the 'earthly' people have understood the vital importance of beauty."

And I closed the address with the following: "Not on snowy heights, but in the turmoil of the city we pronounce these words. And realizing the path of true reality we greet the future with a happy smile."

These words were based on forty years' experience. Ten more years have elapsed since then. Have the formulae then expressed changed during the period? No, the experience of many countries has confirmed and even strengthened them. We must base our conclusions on experience, and on nothing else. Theory for us is only the consequence of practice, and that same practice brings forth the happy smile with which we greet the future. May the smile of knowledge and courage become the banner of our meetings. We unite to apply knowledge; may each crumb of knowledge add spirit to our smile.

How are we to bring art into everyday life? Where are these blessed paths? Perhaps they are inaccessibly difficult? Or they may require enormous wealth? Or perhaps only spiritual giants might venture along these paths of beauty?

All assurances will be unconvincing. These doubts can be answered only by a page out of real life.

I shall take the portraits of four of my friends. They have all left us now. Only one of them was wealthy, the other three were rich only in the brightness of their spirits.

The rich collector was the Moscow merchant Tretiakov. There was nothing in his family to dispose him towards art. Rather, that old merchant family looked with suspicion on the art it did not understand. But unexpectedly young Tretiakov was drawn into a new path, and with uncertainty, guided by personal feeling, he began to collect pictures of the Russian school. He went his way alone, only now and again listening to the advice of some artist friend. And it was not by chance that the now famous Tretiakov Gallery in Moscow began to come into being. With the true intuition of a lover of paintings, Tretiakov understood that the Government generally filled its museums mainly with official productions, passing over the best work of the artists. This official physiognomy of the museums could not reflect the evolution of the national school. So has it been ever since; so far I fear it will be in the future.

Art has always blossomed with an ardent personal urge which will comprehend, find, preserve and give to the whole nation. And thus the merchant Tretiakov grasped the national task of art. He found fresh artistic talents and lightened their path. He preserved their work, surrounding them with pure delight. But he made his joy a national joy, and while still alive, gave his entire remarkable collection to the city of Moscow. The task which he had set for himself was no small one. He had not simply gathered together a mass of valuable pictures, but he made his collection reflect the whole of the Russian school. Everything that was new, brilliant, important came under the eye of Tretiakov. This taciturn, gray-haired man, in his large fur coat, indefatigably visited all exhibitions. Nothing could stop him when he considered a picture important. He would mount the steep stairs leading to the studio of the young beginner in art. He was first to see a picture finished. He was first at the opening of the exhibition. But he was also first to possess the best and most characteristic works.

It came to pass that the prizes given by the highest art institutions were considered as insignificant compared with the purchase of a picture by Tretiakov. The destiny of the beginner in art was decided not by the Academy, but by this sincere and taciturn man. When there was no more room on the walls in his house, Tretiakov built another beside it. If this was needed it had to be done. Art was not to suffer any loss.

Of course it may be said that, given Tretiakov's great wealth, it was possible to collect on this vast scale. He was able to choose the best and could gather enough to represent the whole of the Russian school in his collection. It was true that his wealth made this scale possible, but the quality of the collection, his love of the work, and his living creative work in the choice itself of pictures and of men—all this proceeded not from the amount of his wealth, but from the untold riches of his spirit. Thus did one man, strong in spirit, do an infinitely important national work. Now, should the Government seek to establish a new Tretiakov Gallery, it would find itself powerless to do so, for it was the urge of the spirit that created that inimitable combination of beauty.

This is an instance of ideal creativeness within national limits.

Now for another spiritual portrait. Here we have the same power of a spiritual urge along with a mighty struggle with means. It was Count Golenishtchev-Koutouzov, a well-known poet and worker in the sphere of culture, and the Chamberlain at the Imperial Court. In his case, family traditions led him to develop a love of art. His historical knowledge was great, and he also had special, deep poetic gifts.

His collection consisted of pictures of the old Dutch, Flemish and Italian schools. Its fundamental characteristic was not the search for the conventional names but the truth shown in wonderful creations. The collector understood that the names of Rembrandt, Rubens, Van Dyke were purely collective names that only the lowest type of collector sought in the dark for that which was but an empty sound to him. But a better knowledge of art shows us a countless number of artists who were engulfed in the so-called great names. The task of the cultured collector is to distinguish among these forgotten names for truth's sake. If within an excellent picture attributed to Rembrandt we find the signature of Karl Fabricius, his pupil, is this fine picture any the worse for that? Or again could Van Dyke paint two thousand portraits in one year? Of course not, but he had up to two hundred pupils.

I know how grieved the Count would be to learn that one of his favorite pictures by an unknown Flemish painter Haselaer, now hangs in the Metropolitan Museum in New York under the name of Joachim Patinir.

In the name of truth, Count Golenishtchev-Koutouzov sought to discover the real names of painters and remedied, as far as he could, the sins of mercenary human history. And what loving intimacy breathed out from his choice collection. Every new member of the collection was greeted with the disapproval of numerous relatives who begrudged the money spent on it. Money was so scarce since his small Court salary was not enough to live on. This collector departed this world surrounded by his real friends, his pictures, and he willed that his collection be dispersed to give new joy to new seeking souls.

Golenishtchev-Koutouzov was the type of refined collector who, working and rejoicing in new beauty and truth, then sends it forth again to serve for the ennobling of the human spirit.

Now for the type of a young collector—an instinctive collector who, from his school days develops a love for works of art instead of choosing the joys natural to his age. From childhood, without possessing any personal artistic capabilities, he is distinguished by education and refined taste. He is attracted to all that is beautiful. His spirit seeks to rise.

What pleasure it was to pass the time with young Sleptsov. While yet a pupil of the Imperial Lyceum, he began to collect pictures. His purchases were not chaotic, not accidental. He knew what he was doing. And all the money given to the boy by his mother for pleasures was spent on his noble pursuit. And if sometimes he was short of money, his enthusiasm for his general task never suffered because of this.

And this general task was a fine one. The boy developed a love for certain, very subtly selected painters, and decided to have specimens of each of them in all the periods of their work to preserve and to pass on to posterity a complete picture of the creative human life of each artist. The youth dreamed of the future; each painter was to have a separate room and the whole furnishing of the room was to correspond with the character of the art represented in it— the furniture, the embellishment of the walls and ceiling, the character of the lighting and floor covering. From this we may gather what subtlety of perception lay in that young soul, and what deep love and care surrounded each of the artists represented. In these special rooms, choice singing and music were to be heard at times, or suitable passages were to be read aloud. In a word the dream of Harmony of the Unity of Art was to be realized.

It was a joy to hear how a new work of art was selected for the collection. What subtle and truthful considerations were expressed for discovering and bringing out a new and worthy feature in the creative work of an artist. And you could see no mere fancy in this treatment of art, but a real cultural need. And this subtlety of culture influenced those surrounding him. Both thought and speech were purified by this bright ascension of the spirit.

Sleptsov dreamed of handing over his collection to the nation, without any care for his name. But he left us too early to do so. And he left us in an unusual way. He went out for a ride and did not return. He passed over unexpectedly, in the midst of Nature, listening to the harmony of the Cosmos. An enviable passage—a passage to new beautiful labors.

This was the type of a sensitive soul with ingrained feelings of a future harmony and unity.

Now for one more touching type of a collector.

A very poor officer in a line regiment, stationed in a distant provincial town, reaches out to art with all his soul. Depriving himself of many things Colonel Kratchkovsky, always pleasant in manner, always active, burning with enthusiasm, seeks to gather a collection of specimens of Russian painting. Of course he is unable to collect large pictures so he collects small pictures, sketches, studies, drawings. But his collection becomes a very considerable one in its essential value. He looks for the best painters; he understands that often the sketch is more valuable than the picture itself. He seeks to bring out the character of the artist in its most typical features. This is not a buyer of cheap pictures; this is a true collector. He himself is often in need of ten rubles (five dollars) and for him it is a matter of the greatest consequence whether he has to pay ten rubles more or less for a picture. He asks the painter to let him have the picture and persistently persuades him to lower the price. His words produced their effects and the sketches were given to him; he would rejoice with the bright joy of a child, and would write enthusiastic letters about his new treasure. How he loved art, and with what lofty meaning he surrounded the conception of true creative work.

In his will he bequeathed his entire collection to the public. More than that, he commanded that all his modest property, all that he had in his daily life, be sold and the proceeds applied to the purchase of more works of art which were to be added to his collection.

This is the type of an outwardly unnoticed but deeply important worker for the culture of the future. His example drew the attention of many, and if you could see his letters written from the battlefield! He was a pure soul. Colonel Kratchkovsky left us during the last war.

I might show you many more characters, full of noble seeking in different areas of art, but even these four types show the level of those cultural aspirations which are so necessary for humanity. Thus do things happen, not in dreams, but in real life—sincerely and actively, and such pure labors are accompanied by a smile of joy. How close are the seekings of art to the attainment of the spirit.

It is time to understand, note and to apply these wondrous channels to life.

And when art has entered actively, irresistibly and simply into all spiritual development of public life, then it will be brought also into all of modern life.

And it is through these channels that the true paths of blessing will draw near to every human heart.

REALIZATION OF THE BEAUTIFUL

P LATO ordained in his treatises on statesmanship: "It is difficult to imagine a better method of education than the one that has been discovered and verified by the experience of centuries; it can be expressed in two propositions: gymnastics for the body and music for the soul. In view of this, one must consider education in music as the most important; thanks to it, Rhythm and Harmony are deeply enrooted into the soul, dominate it, fill it with beauty and transform man into a beautiful thinker. . . . He will partake of the Beautiful and rejoice in it, gladly realize it, become saturated with it and will arrange his life in conformity with it."

Of course the word music, in this case, should not be understood as routine musical education as it is understood now in its narrow sense. In Athens, as service to all Muses, music had a far deeper and broader meaning than it does today. This conception embraced not only the harmony of sound, but the whole realm of poetry, the whole domain of elevated perceptions, of exquisite forms, and of creation in general, in its best sense. The great service to the Muses was a real education of taste, which in everything cognizes the great Beautiful. And we shall have to return to this vital Beauty, unless Ideas of elevated constructiveness are to be completely rejected by Humanity.

Hippias Maior (beauty) of the dialogue of Plato is not a vague abstraction, but verily the most vital noble concept. Beauty exists in itself! It is sensed and realized. In this realization is contained an inspiring, encouraging call to the study and implanting of all the covenants of the beautiful. "The philosophical morale" of Plato is animated by the sense of the beautiful. Did Plato himself, who was sold into slavery because of the hatred of the tyrant Dionysius, not prove, later on, by his own example the vitality of the beautiful path when he was re-established and living in the gardens of the Academy,? Of course Plato's gymnastics were not the coarse football or anti-cultural breaking of noses of modern prize-fights. The gymnastics of Plato were the same gates to the Beautiful, the discipline of Harmony and uplifting of the body into the spiritual spheres.

Not once have we spoken about the introduction in school of a Chair of Living Ethics, a course in the Art of Thinking. Without the education for the general realization of the Beautiful, these two courses will again remain a dead letter. Again in the course of only a few years, the lofty and vital principles of ethics will turn into a dead dogma if they will not be imbued with the Beautiful.

Many vital concepts of antiquity have become belittled and vulgar in our household, instead of their deserved expansion. Thus the wide and lofty service to the Muses has turned into a narrow conception of playing one instrument. When you hear nowadays the word music, you imagine first of all a lesson of music often with conventional limitations. When you hear the word Museum one understands it as a storeroom of all kinds of art objects. As with every store-house, this conception creates a certain flavor of deadliness. Such limited conceptions of the word Museum, as a storage place, so deeply entered our understanding, that when one pronounces this concept in its original meaning—Muzeon—then no one understands what is really meant. Yet every Hellene of even average education would at once know that Muzeon means first of all the home of Muses.

Foremost all Muzeon is the abode of all aspects of the Beautiful; not at all in the sense of only storing different kinds of art creations, but in the sense of the most vital and creative application of them in life. Thus nowadays one often hears that people express surprise when a Museum, as such, occupies itself with all spheres of art, with the education of good taste and with the spreading of the feeling for the Beautiful.

In this regard we recall the Covenants of Plato. So likewise we might have recalled Pythagoras with his "Laws about the Beautiful," with his steadfast foundations of resplendent universal affirmations. The ancient Hellenes reached such a level of sensitivity that they proclaimed their Pantheon as an Altar to the Unknown God. In this ascent of the Spirit, they approach the inexpressible finesse of the understanding of the ancient Hindus who, on pronouncing "Neti, Neti", did not thereby express something negative, but quite the opposite. In saying "Not That, Not That" they were pointing out the indescribable grandeur of an Unutterable Concept. It is significant that such great conceptions were not abstract, as if living only in the mind and reason; no, they dwelled in the very heart, as something living, life bringing, inalienable and indestructible, as defined so beautifully in the Bhagvad Gita. In the heart that sacred fire was aflame which was at the base of all flaming commandments also of the hermits of Mt. Sinai. The same sacred fire moulded the precious images of St. Theresa, St. Francis, St. Sergius and all Fathers of the "Love of the Good," who knew so much and were understood so little.

We speak of the education of good taste as of a matter of truly basic world significance of every country. When we speak about vital ethics which should become the favorite school hour of every child, we appeal to the contemporary heart, pleading to it for expansion if even only to the extent of ancient ordainments.

Can one consider as natural the fact that the conception so glorified already in the time of Pythagoras and Plato, has become so limited now and has lost its actual meaning after all the ages of so-called progress? Pythagoras already, in the fifth century B.C., symbolized in himself the whole harmonious "Pythagorean Life." It was Pythagoras who affirmed music and astronomy as sisters sciences. Pythagoras who was called a charlatan by bigots, must be horrified to see how, instead of a harmonious development, our contemporary life has been broken up and mutilated, and that we do not even understand the meaning of the beautiful hymn to the sun—to Light.

Today very strange formulas sometimes appear in the press. For instance, the flourishing of the intellect is the sign of degeneration. A very strange formula, if only the author does not attribute some special narrow meaning to the word intellect. Of course if the word intellect is only taken as being the expression of the conventional, withered mind, then to some extent, this formula may have its foundation. But it is dangerous in case the author does understand intellect as intelligence, which first of all should be connected to the education of good taste as the most vital principle of life.

Quite recently, before our eyes in the West, the new word—intelligentsia has been adopted. In the beginning, this newcomer was met rather suspiciously, but soon it was adopted in literature. It would be important to determine whether this expression symbolizes the intellect, or if, according to the ancient conceptions, it corresponds to the education of good taste.

If it is a symbol of refined and expanded consciousness then we have to greet this innovation, which perhaps will remind us once more of ancient beautiful principles.

In my letter "Synthesis", the difference between the concepts of Culture and Civilization was discussed. Both these concepts are sufficiently separated even in standard dictionaries. Therefore let us not return to these two sequential concepts, even if someone would be content with the conception of civilization without dreaming about the higher concept of culture.

But having remembered the concept of the "intelligentsia" it will be permissible to ask, whether this concept belongs to Civilization, as an expression of intellect, or does it also embrace the highest step? To be exact, does it enter into the state of Culture, in which the heart and the spirit also act? Of course, if we would suppose that the word "intelligentsia" refers only to the stage of reason, then it would hardly be worthwhile to introduce it as a new usage. One may admit an innovation where it introduces something new, or at least sufficiently revitalizes the ancient principles within the frame of the present day.

Of course everyone will agree that intelligentsia, this aristocracy of the Spirit, belongs to Culture and only in this connection one could greet this new literary expression.

In this case the education of good taste belongs, of course, first of all to the intelligentsia, and not only does it belong, but it becomes its duty. Not fulfilling this duty, intelligentsia has no right to its existence and condemns itself to savagery.

The education of taste cannot be an abstraction. First of all, this is a vital achievement in all the domains of life, for otherwise where can the boundary of service to the muses as practiced by the ancient Hellenes be set? If the ancients understood this service in its entire scope and the application to life of these beautiful principles, should we not feel humiliated to clip the luminous wings of the fiery radiant angels through prejudice and bigotry!

When we suggest ethics as a subject for the schools, a subject most interesting, vast, full of creative principles, we thus offer the reformation of taste, as a fortification against ugliness.

Andromeda said, "I brought thee Fire." And the ancient Hellenes, following Euripides, understood what Fire it was, and why it was so precious. But we in the majority of cases utilize these inspiring words of guidance like a phosphorous match. We think of the high concept of phosphorous, the carrier of Light, only as a match by which we ignite our cold hearth in order to cook our daily gruel. And where is tomorrow, this luminous, wonderful Tomorrow?

We have forgotten about it. We have forgotten it because we have lost our quests. We have lost our refined tastes which propel us toward improvement, aspiration and consciousness. Aspirations have become for us passing dreams; but the one who does not know how to aspire, does not belong to the future life, does not belong to the human kinship of a higher image.

Even the simple truth that the first distinction between man and beast is the former's capacity to dream of the future has already become trite. But the truism itself has not become the commonly-accepted truth as it should be, but only a synonym for truth about which one need not think. Nevertheless, in spite of everything, in times of even the greatest difficulties, let us not postpone or delay anything concerning the education of taste. Let us not delay our thoughts on the subject of Light-bearing Ethics. Let us not forget about the art of thinking and let us remember about the treasure of the heart.

"A certain hermit left his retreat and came with the message, saying to everyone: 'Thou hast a heart.'

When he was asked why he does not speak about mercy, patience, devotion, love and all other benevolent foundations of life, he replied 'If they only do not forget the heart, the rest will adjust itself! Verily can we appeal for love, if it has no place to reside? And where could patience dwell, when its abode is closed? Thus, in order not to be tormented by goodness unapplied, one must create a garden for it, which will flourish in the midst of the realization of the heart.. Let us stand firmly on the foundation of the heart and let us understand that without the heart we are as a perishable shell." Thus the wise ones ordained. Thus ordains Agni Yoga. Thus let us accept and apply.

Without the untiring realization of the Beautiful, without incessant refinement of the heart and consciousness, we would make the laws of earthly existence cruel and deadly in their hatred against humanity. In other words, we would, by killing the Beautiful, help contribute to the most shameful, debased destruction.

The Romans said: *Sub pretextu juris summum jus saepe summa injuria; suaviter in modo fortifer in re.* (Under pretext of justice a strict application of law is often the gravest injury. Be gentle in manner thou, resolute in execution).

Let us be broad and resolute in the realization of the Beautiful!

Vivekananda said: "The artist is a witness of the Beautiful."

Rabindranath Tagore finishes his book *What is Art?* with such words: "In Art the person in us is sending its answer to the Supreme Person who reveals Himself to us in a world of endless beauty across the lightless world of facts."

There is no other way, O friends scattered! May my call penetrate to you. Let us join ourselves by the invisible threads of the Beautiful. I turn to you, I call to you:

In the name of Beauty and Wisdom, let us combine for struggle and work. During days of Armageddon let us ponder about Eternal Values, which are the cornerstones of Evolution.

In the name of Culture I send you from the Himalayas my heartiest greetings!

THE BEAUTIFUL

"THE artist is the priest of the Beautiful. It is he who rescues the truth from its ugly defilement and allows us to drink of the perennial fount of joy amidst the fret and stress of life."

"The beautiful is scattered throughout the universe like the auriferous sands!"

So writes Bhabes Chandra Chaudhuri in his article "The Artist and the Beauty in Art."

It is joy to read such an appreciative article in which the artist himself affirms the significance of Beauty. There was a time when it was considered, for some reason, that an artist should not be a writer. Sometimes such artificial preconceptions went so far as to say that a talented composer, according to the judgment of his impresario, should not be permitted to appear in public as a conductor, as it was believed that public opinion would thereby be confused. One can imagine how Leonardo da Vinci, Vasari or Cellini would laugh at such an absurd way of obstructing creative thought.

It seems that in the history of art there are many convincing examples of how people who devoted themselves to Beauty expressed it in a multitude of ways, choosing that which at the moment appeared to them the best way to do so. How beautifully they combined painting with architecture, or with sculpture, not to speak of mosaics and various graphic arts.

As priests they served Beauty, finding the most persuasive expressions for their beneficent influence on the general masses, and for refining the consciousness of the people.

In India today we notice a renaissance of art. There appear glorious hosts of artists. State Galleries are being opened, and frescoes again adorn public buildings. The best artists are heading Art Schools, and art is sure to be found in many monthly journals and magazines. The artificial barriers between so-called "great art" and "applied art" are breaking down. Verily Beauty is great in all its variety. It is a pleasure to find a page on art and many reproductions of art both modern and ancient in many monthly journals and magazines.

Someone may smile and think: "This sounds very encouraging, but what of the difficult life artists lead?" Of course their lives are not easy, nor is any heroic achievement. No one will think that the lives of Rembrandt or Rubens were easy. It is only in recent times that their names have become great collective concepts above any doubts. But we know that the beautiful masterpieces of Rembrandt which he was commissioned to paint were rejected by the local authorities and municipalities. We also know that Leonardo in Florence and Michel Angelo in Rome experienced great hardships. Time adorns all sufferings with epic beatitude and calm. Yet how many tragedies remain hidden behind the gorgeous brocaded curtains of Time.

We all know the martyrdom of scientists like Copernicus, Galileo, Paracelsus, Lavoisier and innumerable other sufferers for truth. There exist entire books dedicated to these martyrs of Science. And next to them there should also exist volumes entitled "Martyrs of Art and Culture." However, once we know that artists are priests of the Beautiful, we also know that the attainment of all other attributes is inevitable.

Much has been written about vandalism. We introduced the Banner of Peace as a Red Cross of Culture to protect real treasures of humanity. And now let me mention another hidden but cruel vandalism, which quietly exists in the life of many nations.

When studying old masters, we often come across the fact that many very good paintings were for some reason overpainted with entirely different subjects by inferior artists. It is obvious that the old painting had become old-fashioned and the artist simply used the wood as material for his modern and more fashionable expressions. One should not think that only paintings of secondary importance were subjected to such barbaric manipulations. On the contrary, amongst the recorded cases we find some very important ones which today occupy a place of honor in the history of art.

I remember how once in Italy while studying a beautiful painting "Virgo Inter Virgines," we were surprised at its exceptionally good condition. When expressing our amazement at this, we received the following unusual but characteristic explanation: "Apparently at the beginning of the 17th Century this beautiful painting was already considered old-fashioned and therefore, despite the religious subject, it was covered by another religious subject, 'Ecce Homo,' and had remained all the time in a certain monastery. This second painting was by far inferior to the original masterpiece. It was noticed comparatively recently that the outlines of a different composition were becoming vaguely discernible through the second painting, and the person who had purchased this inexpensive painting from the monastery decided to remove the upper layer, thus revealing a beautiful masterpiece." Now this painting adorns the Art Institute in Chicago.

I have also personally seen an old replica of the well-known painting by Corregio which is in the National Gallery in London. On this replica I could clearly see the outlines of an ancient portrait, and indeed the panel on which it was painted proved to be far older than the replica. Once we had occasion to witness how, from beneath paintings of the 17th and 18th centuries beautiful originals appeared in good condition by Lambert, Lombard, Rogier van der Weyden, Adrien Bloemaert and similar renowned artists. In the Bulletin of the Museum of Fine Arts in Boston we find a most instructive story about the portrait of Sir William Butts, by Hans Holbein the Younger. Let us quote a few lines from this article:

"On November 17, 1935, the Museum purchased the striking portrait by Hans Holbein the Younger.... Connoisseurs, seeing the portrait, refused to believe that Holbein could have done it, and with good reason. As it appeared for about three and a half centuries it was certainly not Holbein. In very recent times, however, a young friend of the Butts family which had retained possession of the painting from the time it was done until it passed to the Museum, H. M. Jonas, remarked that the hands seemed to be painted in a manner somewhat different from the rest of the portrait and suggested an earlier style. He was permitted to have an X-ray made and the result was the discovery of a portrait underneath. The X-ray showed a different outline to the cap, a full beard, a different chain and a suit puffed with white silk. It also revealed the existence of an inscription on the background. Next came the difficulty of the restoration. The first restoration was undertaken by Nico Jungman. It was an extremely difficult task, since the overpainting was of very nearly the same period as the painting underneath. It is obvious that the sitter caused his portrait to be repainted later in life. We cannot be sure when this was done, though it was probably in 1563 when Queen Elizabeth came to Thornage and was elaborately feted. It is likely that then, Sir William, an old man holding high offices, demanded that he be shown with different garments and ornaments added, and therefore had himself repainted, presented in regalia and brought up-to-date, but unfortunately by a very inferior artist."

This interesting story has two corollaries. First, we must pay tribute to the administration of the Boston Museum of Fine Arts and to the restorer, who have completed this most difficult restoration so successfully, and thus have revealed to the world the original masterpiece of a great artist without any later inferior additions and overpainting. Secondly, this instructive historical episode shows to us once more that vandalism is committed not only by the hands of an infuriated mob but also tacitly in highly distinguished dwellings for the sake of vanity and prejudice.

Beauty cannot be guarded by orders and laws alone. Only when human consciousness realizes the inestimable value of beauty—creating, ennobling and refining —only then will the real treasures of humanity be safe. And one should not think that vandalisms, obvious or tacit, belong only to past ages, to some fabulous invaders and conquerors. We see vandalism of many kinds taking place even today. Therefore the endeavour to protect and save beauty is not an abstract nebulous move, but is imperative, real and undeferrable.

Verily education in art and beauty is a necessity with all its duties and obligations. We always rejoice when we see that thoughts are being transmuted into action. It is for this reason that the opening of new schools, the inauguration of an International Academy of the Arts, is always to be greatly welcomed.

Twenty years ago we wrote upon the shields of the Master Institute of United Arts and of the International Art Centre the following mottoes:

Art will unify all humanity. Art is one—indivisible. Art has its many branches, yet all are one. Art is the manifestation of the coming synthesis. Art is for all. Everyone will enjoy true art. The gates of the "sacred source" must be wide open for everybody, and the light of art will influence numerous hearts with a new love. At first this feeling will be unconscious, but afterwards it will purify human consciousness. How many young hearts are searching for something real and beautiful! So, give it to them. Bring art to the people—where it belongs. We should have not only museums, theaters, universities, public libraries, railway stations and hospitals, but even prisons decorated and beautified. Then we shall have no more prisons.

Humanity is facing the coming events of cosmic greatness. Humanity already realizes that no occurrences are accidental. The time for the construction of future culture is at hand. Before our eyes re-evaluation of values is being witnessed. Amidst ruins of valueless banknotes, mankind has found the real value of the world's significance. The values of great art are victoriously traversing all storms of earthly commotions. Even the "earthly" people already understand the vital importance of beauty that is alive. And when we proclaim love, beauty and action, we know verily that we pronounce the formula, of the International language. And this formula which belongs to the museum and stage must enter daily life. The sign of beauty will open all sacred gates. Beneath the sign of beauty we walk joyfully. With beauty we conquer. Through beauty we pray. In beauty we are united. And now we affirm these words—not on the snowy heights, but amidst the turmoil of the city. And realizing the path of true reality, we greet the future with a happy smile.

Twenty years have elapsed and we see that all the requirements of Beauty have become still more urgent. Everything that has been done in this direction still remains as if it were on isolated islands. Beauty does not tolerate conventional limitations and boundaries. The treasures of beauty belong to the world. Hence the care for art and knowledge is also a universal duty on a planetary scale.

Culture—the veneration of Light—rests on the cornerstones of Beauty and Knowledge. And if there was a beautiful necessity to inaugurate the Red Cross of Culture and a universal Banner reminding men of the treasures of Culture—it means that this beautiful necessity also was undeferrable. Culture, Beauty and Science are violated not only in times of war, but also in times of so-called peace. This truth again refers to the whole world.

If anyone should possess a receptacle containing a wonderful panacea, how carefully would he guard such a treasure. But beauty is that same miracle-working panacea and as such requires a vigilant devotion. Now cures are affected in hospitals by sound and color—thus Beauty, the perfect panacea, enters in a new garment. People worry about their health. May this consideration at least teach them to venerate and guard the panacea of Beauty. Half a century ago our great Dostoyevsky proclaimed: "Beauty will save the world."

Amidst the touching definitions of art I recollect two legends, one from Chinese Turkestan, the other from Tibet.

An artist wanted some money for his painting and when he came to the moneylender, the man was absent and only a boy was there. This boy gave the artist a very large sum for the painting. When the moneylender came back, he said: "For these fruits and vegetables you gave such a great sum!" and he discharged the boy. Time passed and the artist returned and asked for the painting. When he saw it he was horrified, saying: "That is not my painting. Where are the butterflies? Go find the boy that he may help us find my painting. This painting you show me has only cabbages." The boy came and said: "Now it is winter, and the butterflies come only in the summer time. Put the painting near the fire, and we shall see the butterflies return." And so it was; the paint was put on the canvas so skilfully that during the cold weather the colors receded, but in the warmth they returned. Thus do the people of Kuchar speak beautifully about the perfection of art.

And the other from Tibet: Why do the giant trumpets in the Buddhist temples have such a resonant tone? The ruler of Tibet decided to summon from India, from the place where the Blessed One dwelled, a great Teacher, in order to purify the fundamentals of teaching. How to meet the esteemed guest?

Gold and precious gems would not be adequate to meet a spiritual Teacher. Then the High Lama of Tibet, having had a vision, gave the design for a new giant trumpet so that the guest could be received with unprecedented majestic sound; and the meeting was a wonderful one—not with the wealth of gold but with the grandeur of the beautiful sound.

The master could be greeted only with something beautiful: The sense of the beautiful must be that life-giving seed—that real panacea, which makes the deserts, both physical and spiritual, flourish.

And from where else can a sense of Goodwill and Unity come if not through the Blessed realization of the Beautiful!

TREASURE OF THE HOME

O NE recalls an incident: Two visitors are In the office of a certain president. The walls of the old room are decorated with massive oak bookcases. Through the glass panels temptingly glow the backs with their rich bindings. Although the bindings are not old, they are heavily gold-leaved. Apparently here is a lover of books. How splendid that at the head of this undertaking there is a collector who has not spared money on his alluring bindings.

One of the visitors yields to the temptation of turning the leaves and holding this treasure of the spirit in his hands. The bookcase is apparently unlocked and raising his hand the booklover attempts to take one of the volumes. But, oh, horror! the entire shelf falls on his head, revealing that these are false bindings without any sign of a book. His most sensitive wish violated, the booklover with trembling hands, replaces this unworthy imitation upon its shelf: "Let us get away from here as soon as possible. Can one expect anything decent from such a clown?!" The other visitor smiles. "Here one is punished for loving books: Because it is a happiness not only to read a good book, but even to hold it in one's hands."

How many such false libraries are spread all over the world? And whom do their owners presume to cheat—their own friends or themselves? In this falsification lies hidden an unusually subtle disdain of knowledge and a refined insult towards the book as the witness of human achievement. And not only are the contents of the book being violated, but in such falsifications, objective as well as in words, the very significance of the creation of the spirit is being assaulted.

"Tell me who are your enemies and I will tell you who you are," said the ancients. One may say: "Show me your bookcase and I will tell you who you are."

One of the most exhausting tasks is the search for a new apartment. But through this involuntary intrusion into numerous dwellings, you undoubtedly discover observations about the facts of life. You pass through numerous apartments of approximate wealth which are not yet filled with furniture. But where is the bookcase? Where is the writing desk? Why are the rooms sometimes overcrowded with such strange ugly objects, yet these two friends of existence—a writing desk and a bookcase are lacking? Is there a place to put them? It appears upon examination that a small desk could still be placed somewhere but the walls are all so covered, that there is no place for a bookcase.

Every librarian is a friend of the artist and scientist. The librarian is the first messenger of Beauty and Knowledge. It is he who opens the gates and from the dead shelves extracts the hidden word to enlighten the searching mind. Not one catalogue may replace a librarian. A loving word and experienced hand may produce the miracle of enlightenment. We affirm that beauty and knowledge are the basis of the entire culture, and these are changing the whole history of humanity. This is not a dream. We can prove it through all of history. The immutable facts tell us how, from primitive ages, all progress, all happiness, all enlightenment of humanity was led by Beauty and Knowledge.

It is not strange to speak these words at a time when millions of books are printed; every year a torrent of printed pages forms new snowy mountains. In this labyrinth of paper glaciers, true snow blindness can strike the inexperienced traveler. But the librarian, as a true honor guard of knowledge, is vigilant. Only he knows how to steer the boat through the waves of this ocean of past and future.

The library exists not only to spread knowledge. Each library is an introduction to bringing knowledge into the home. Is it possible to imagine a home and a household without books? Again, if you will take the most ancient images of the home and household, the finest examples revealed are objects and books. And you can see that these old books, in their beautiful bindings, were held as a true treasure. And not because the library did not exist. Librarians existed throughout the ages. But the human spirit feels that knowledge can be acquired, not only in public places, but also in the calm of the home. We even carry the most sacred books and images with us. They are our unchangeable friends and guides. We know perfectly that it is not worthwhile to read a book once. As magical signs, the truth and beauty of the book is absorbed gradually. And we do not know either the day or the hour when we need the gospel of knowledge. So, the library is the first step of enlightenment. But the true upliftment of knowledge comes in the hour of silence, in solitude when we can concentrate all our intelligence towards the true meaning of scriptures.

Books are true friends of humanity and each human being is entitled to have these noble possessions. In the East, in the wise East, a book is the most precious gift. And he who gives the gift of a book is regarded as a noble man. During five years of travel in Asia we have seen innumerable libraries in each monastery, in every temple, in every ruined Chinese watch tower. There was a library with collections of the most remarkable books—and collections of famous biographies, dictionaries, history and the sciences.

When you see a lonely traveler in the mountains, you may be sure that a book is in his knapsack. You may deprive him of everything, he will be resigned to it, but he will fight for his real treasure, the book.

So, let us remember that books are real treasures and let us collect and cherish them as the noble crest of our home.

GURU—THE TEACHER

ONCE in Karelia I sat on the shores of Lake Ladoga with a farm lad. A middle-aged man passed us by and my small companion stood up and with great reverence took off his cap. I asked him after, "Who was this man?" And with special seriousness, the boy answered, "He is a teacher." I again asked, "Is he your teacher?" "No," answered the boy, "he is the teacher from the neighboring school." "Then you know him personally?" I persisted. "No," he answered, with astonishment. . . . "Then why did you respect him with such reverence?" Still more seriously my little companion answered, "Because he is a teacher."

An almost similar incident happened to me on the banks of the Rhine. Again with joyous amazement I saw how a young man greeted a school teacher. I recall the most uplifting memories of my teacher, Professor Kuindzhi, the famous Russian artist. His life story could fill the most inspiring pages of a biography for the young generation. He was a simple shepherd boy in the Crimea. Only by incessant, ardent effort towards art was he able to conquer all obstacles and finally become, not only a highly-esteemed artist and a man of great means, but also a real Guru for his pupils in the high Hindu conception.

Three times he tried to enter the Imperial Academy of Fine Arts and three times he was refused. The third time, twenty-nine competitors were admitted and not one of them left his name in the history of art. But only one, Kuindzhi, was refused. The Council of the Academy was not made up of Gurus, and certainly was short-sighted. But the young man was persistent and instead of uselessly trying, he painted a landscape and presented it to the Academy for Exhibition. He received two honors without passing the examination. From early morning he worked, but at noon he climbed up to the terraced roof of his house in Petrograd, where, with the shot marking each midday, thousands of birds completely surrounded him. He fed them, speaking to them, studying them as a loving father. Sometimes, very rarely, he invited us, his disciples, to his famous roof, and we heard remarkable stories about the personalities of the birds, about their individual habits and the ways to approach them. At this moment, this short stocki-ly-built man with his leonine head, became as gentle as Saint Francis. Once I saw him very downcast during the entire day. One of his beloved butterflies had broken its wing and he had invented some very skilful means to mend it, but this invention was too heavy and he had been unsuccessful in this noble effort.

But with his pupils and artists, he knew how to be firm. Very often he repeated: "If you are an artist, even in prison, you shall become one." Once a man came to his studio with some very fine sketches and stud-ies. Kuindzhi praised them. But the man said: "Well I am unfortunate because I cannot afford to continue painting." "Why?" Kuindzhi asked compassionately, and the man said that he had a family to support and was employed from ten to six. Then Kuindzhi asked him piercingly: "And from four to ten in the morning, what do you do?" "When?" asked the man. Kuindzhi explained, "Certainly in the morning." "In the morning I sleep," answered the man. Kuindzhi raised his voice and said. "Well, you shall sleep away your entire life. Don't you know that four to nine is the best creative time? And it is not necessary to work on your art more than five hours a day." Then Kuindzhi added; "When I worked as a retoucher in a photographic studio, I also had my job from ten to six. But from four to nine I had quite enough time to become an artist."

Sometimes, when the pupil dreamed about some special conditions for his work, Kuindzhi laughed. "If you are so delicate that you have to be put in a glass case, then better perish as soon as possible, because our life does not need such an exotic plant." But when he saw that his disciple conquered circumstances and went victoriously through the ocean of earthstorms, his eyes sparkled and in full voice, he shouted. "Neither sun nor frost can destroy you. This is the way. If you have something to say you will be able to manifest your message in spite of all the conditions in the world."

I recall how once he came to my studio on the sixth floor, which at that time was without an elevator, and severely criticized my painting. Thus, he left practically nothing of my original conception, and in much uproar he went away. But in less than half an hour, I heard his heavy steps again, and he knocked on the door. Again he had climbed up the long steps in his heavy fur coat, and said: "Well, I hope you shall not take everything I said seriously. Everyone can have his point of view. I felt badly when I realized that perhaps you took all of our discussion too seriously. Everything can be approached in different ways, and really, truth is infinite."

And sometimes, in the greatest secrecy, he entrusted one of his disciples to bring some money anonymously from him to some of the poorest students. And he entrusted this only when he was completely confident that this secret would not be revealed. It happened once that in the academy, revolt against the Vice President Count Tolstoy arose, and as no one could calm the anger of the students, the situation became very serious. Then finally Kuindzhi arrived at the general meeting, and everyone became silent. He said: "Well I am no judge. I do not know if your cause is just or not, but I personally ask you to begin your work because you have come here to be artists." The meeting was ended at once, and everyone returned to the classrooms, because Kuindzhi himself had asked. Such was the authority of the Guru.

I do not know from where this conception of real Guruship arose in the refined Eastern understanding. Certainly he expressed it sincerely, without any superficial intention. This was his style and in the sincerity of this style, he conquered not only as an artist but also as a powerful vital type who gave his disciples the same broad inflexible power to reach their goal.

Long afterwards in India, I saw such figures of Gurus and I have seen the faithful disciples who without any servile obeisance, but rather with great enthusiasm of spirit, venerated their Gurus with that full sensitivity of thought which is so characteristic of India.

Our responsibility before the Beautiful is great! If we feel it, we can demand the same responsibility to this highest principle from our pupils. If we know that this is a necessity, as during an ocean storm, we can require of our companions the same attention to the ardent demand of the moment.

We are introducing, by all means, art into all manifestations of life. We are striving to show the quality of creative labor, but this quality can be recognized only when we know what ecstasy is experienced before the beautiful; this ecstasy is not that of a transfixed image, but is motion, an all-vibrating Nirvana. This is not only the falsely-conceived Nirvana of immobility, but the Nirvana of the noblest and most intensive activity. In all ancient teachings, we have heard about the nobility of action. How can these actions be noble, if they are not beautiful? You are the teachers of art; you are the emissaries of beauty; you know the responsibility before the coming generation and in this is manifested your joy and your invincible power. Your actions are the noble actions.

And to you, my young unseen friends, we are sending out our call. We know how difficult it is for you to begin the struggle for light and achievement. But the obstacles are only new possibilities to create beneficent energy. Without battle, there is no victory. And how can you avoid the venomous arrows of the dark enemy? By approaching your enemy so closely that he shall lack space even to send an arrow. And after all, nothing enlightened may be achieved without travail. So blessed be labor. And blessed be you, young friends, who are walking in victory! The Gurus of the past and future are with you.

Gurus, to you my invocation and my reverence!

CULTURAL UNITY

OUR Times are verily difficult, because of all the commotions, all the lack of understanding and all attacks of darkness against Light. Quite recently there were pictures in magazines showing the auto-da-fé of precious books in the streets. It is hard to realize that this could have taken place in the present age, after millions of years of the existence of our planet. But perhaps this terrible tension is the impulse to direct humanity through all storms and over all abysses to peaceful construction and mutual respect. What an epoch-making day might be before us when over all countries, all centers of spirit, beauty and knowledge, the One Banner of Culture could be unfurled! This sign would call everyone to revere the treasures of human genius, to respect culture and to have a new recognition of labor as the only measure of true values. From childhood, people will witness that there exists not only a flag of human health but there also is a sign of peace and culture for the health of the spirit. This sign, unfurled over all treasures of human genius will say: "Here the treasure of all mankind are guarded; here above all petty divisions, above illusory frontiers of enmity and hatred, the fiery stronghold of love, labor and all-moving creation is towering."

Real Peace, Real Unity is desired by the human heart. It strives to labor creatively and actively for its labor is a source of joy. It wants to love and expand in the realization of Sublime Beauty. In the highest perception of Beauty and Knowledge all conventional divisions disappear. The heart speaks its own language; it wants to rejoice what is common to all, what uplifts all, and what leads to the radiant Future. All symbols and tablets of humanity contain one hieroglyph, the sacred prayer—Peace and Unity.

It is truly beautiful, if amidst the turmoil of life, in the waves of unsolved social problems, we still may hold up before us the eternal flambeau torches of peace in all ages. It is beautiful, through the inexhaustible well of love and tolerance, to understand the great movements which connected the highest knowledge to the highest aspirations. Thus, by studying and admiring we are becoming real cooperators with evolution, and out of the brilliant rays of the Supreme Light may emerge true knowledge. This refined knowledge is based on real comprehension and tolerance. From this source comes the great understanding, emerges the Supremely Beautiful, the enlightenment and enthusiasm for Unity. Contemporary life is changing rapidly, the signs of a new evolution are knocking on all doors. In real, unconventional science we feel the splendid responsibility before the coming generations. We gradually understand the harm of everything negative. We begin to value enlightened positiveness and constructiveness, and in this measure, in merciful tolerance, we can prepare a vital happiness for our next generation, turning vague abstractions into beneficent realities.

On the scrolls of command it has been inscribed that a spiritual garden is in daily need of the same watering as a garden of flowers. If we still consider the physical flowers the true adornment of our life, then how much more must we remember and prescribe to the creative values of the spirit the leading place in the life which surrounds us? Let us then, with untiring eternal vigilance, benevolently mark the manifestations of the workers of culture; and let us strive in every possible way to ease this difficult path of heroic achievement.

Let us also mark and find a place in our lives for the great ones, remembering that their name no longer is personal with all the attributes of the limited ego, but has become the property of pan-human culture, and must be safeguarded and firmly cared for in the most benevolent conditions.

We shall thus continue their self-sacrificing labor and we shall cultivate their creative sowing which, as we see, is so often covered with the dirt of noncomprehension and overgrown with the weeds of ignorance.

As a caring gardener, the true culture-bearer will not forcefully crush those flowers which entered life not from the main road if they belonged to the same precious kinds which he safeguards. The manifestations of culture are just as manifold as are the manifestations of the endless varieties of life itself. They ennoble Be-ness. They are the true branches of the one sacred Tree, whose roots sustain the Universe.

If you shall be asked, of what kind of country and of what kind of future constitution you dream, you can answer with full dignity: The country of Great Culture shall be your noble motto. You shall know that in that country there will be peace, a country where knowledge and beauty will be revered.

Everything created by hostility is impracticable and perishable. The history of mankind gave us remarkable examples of how necessary just peaceful creativeness was for progress. The hand will tire from the sword but the creating hand sustained by the might of the Spirit is untiring and unconquerable. No sword can destroy the heritage of culture. The human mind may temporarily deviate from the primary courses, but at the predestined hour, it will have to return to them with the renewed powers of the spirit.

Culture and Peace make man verily invincible; realizing all spiritual conditions, he becomes tolerant and all-embracing. Each intolerance is but a sign of weakness. If we understand that every lie, every fallacy shall be exposed, it means that, first of all, a lie is stupid and impracticable. But what has he to hide who has consecrated himself to Peace and Culture? Helping what is near to him, he helps the general welfare which was appreciated in all ages. Striving for Peace, he becomes a pillar of a progressing State. Not slandering what is near to us, we increase productiveness. Not quarreling, we shall prove that we possess the knowledge of the foundations. Not wasting time in idleness, we shall prove that we are true co-workers in the plough-field of Culture. Finding joy in daily labor we show that the concept of Infinity is not alien to us. Not harming others, we do not harm ourselves, and in eternally giving we realize that in giving we receive. And this blessed receiving is not a hidden treasure of a miser. We understand how creative is affirmation and how destructive is negation. Amidst basic concept, those of Peace and Culture are the conceptions which even a complete ignoramus will not dare to attack. There where is culture, there is peace. There where is the right solution for the difficult social problems is achievement. Culture is the cumulation of highest Bliss, of highest Beauty, of highest Knowledge.

We are tired of destruction and negations. Positive creativeness is the fundamental quality of the human spirit. Let us welcome all those who, surmounting personal difficulties and casting aside petty selfishness, propel their spirits to the task of preserving culture, thus insuring a radiant future. We must not fear enthusiasm. Only the ignorant and the spiritually impotent would scoff at this noble feeling. Such scoffing is but the sign of inspiration for the true Legion of Honor.

Nothing can impede us from dedicating ourselves to the service of Culture, so long as we believe in it and give it our most ardent thoughts.

Do not disparage! Only in harmony with evolution can we ascend! And nothing can extinguish the selfless and flaming wings of enthusiasm!

ADAMANT

TO the sacred ideals of nations in our days the watchwords: 'Art and Knowledge,' have been added with special imperativeness. It is just now that something must be said of the particular significance of these great conceptions both for the present time and for the future. I address these words to those whose eyes and ears are not yet filled with the rubbish of everyday life, to those whose hearts have not yet been stopped by the lever of the machine called 'Mechanical civilization.'

Art and Knowledge! Beauty and Wisdom! It is not necessary to speak of the eternal and still renewed meaning of these concepts. Every child already instinctively understands the value of decoration and knowledge when but starting on the path of life. Only later, under the grimace of disfigured life this light of the spirit becomes darkened, for while in the kingdom of vulgarity it has no place and is unknown. Yes, the spirit of the age attains even to such monstrosity!

It is not the first time that I have knocked at these gates and I here again appeal to you.

Amongst horrors, in the midst of the struggles and collisions of the people, the questions of knowledge and of art are matters of primary importance. Do not be astonished. This is not an exaggeration, nor is it a platitude. It is an unequivocal affirmation, the only road to Peace.

The question of the relativity of human knowledge has always been much argued. But now, when the whole of mankind has felt, the horrors of war directly or indirectly, this question has become a vital one. People have not only become accustomed to think, but even to speak without shame about things of which they evidently have not the slightest knowledge. On every hand men repeat opinions which are altogether unfounded, and such judgments bring great harm into the world, an irreparable harm.

We must admit that during the last few years, European culture has been shaken to its very foundation. In the pursuit of things whose achievement has not yet been destined to mankind, the fundamental steps of ascent have been destroyed. Humanity has tried to lay hold onto treasures which it has not deserved and thus has rent the benevolent veil of the goddess of happiness.

Of course, what mankind has not yet attained it is destined to attain in due time, but how much man will have to suffer to atone for the destruction of the forbidden gates! With what labor and self-denial shall we have to build up the new foundations of culture!

The knowledge which is locked up in libraries or in the brains of the teachers again penetrates but little into contemporary life. Again it fails to give birth to active work.

Modern life is filled with the animal demands of the body. We come near to the line of the terrible magic circle, and the only way of conjuring its dark guardians and escaping from it is through the talisman of true Knowledge and Beauty.

The time when this will be a necessity is at hand.

Without any false shame, without the contortions of savages, let us confess that we have come very near to barbarism; confession is already a step towards progress.

It matters not that we still wear European clothes and, following our habit, pronounce special words. But the clothes cover savage impulses and the meaning of the words pronounced, although they are often great, touching, and unifying, is now obscured. The guidance of knowledge is lost. People have become accustomed to darkness.

More knowledge! More art! There are not enough of these bases in life, which alone can lead us to the golden age of unity.

The more we know, the more clearly we see our ignorance. But if we know nothing at all, then we cannot even know we are ignorant. That being so, we have no means of advancement and nothing to strive for, and the dark reign of vulgarity is inevitable. The young generations are not prepared to look boldly, with a bright smile, on the blinding radiance of knowledge and beauty. From where then is the knowledge of the reality of things to come? How then are wise mutual relations to arise? From where is unity to emerge, that unity which is the true guarantee of steady forward movement? Only on the basis of true beauty and true knowledge can a sincere understanding be achieved among the nations. The real guide would be the universal language of Knowledge and of the Beauty of art. Only these guides can establish that kindly outlook which is so necessary for future creative work.

The path of animosity, roughness, and abuse will lead us nowhere. Nothing can be built along that path. Does not a conscience still remain in human nature? The real being in man still seeks to attain justice.

Away with darkness, let us do away with malice and treachery. Mankind has already felt enough of the hand of darkness.

Let me tell you, and remind you, these are not platitudes, not mere words. I give voice to the sincere striving of the worker: the only bases of life are Art and Knowledge.

It is just in these hard days of labor, in this time

of suffering, that we must steadily recall these kindly guides. And in our hours of trial let us affirm them with all the power of our spirit.

You say: 'Life is hard. How can we think of knowledge and beauty if we have nothing to live on?" or "we are far away from knowledge and art; we have important business to attend to first."

But I say: You are right, but you are also wrong, Knowledge and art are not luxuries. Knowledge and art are not idleness. It is time to remember this. They are prayer and the work of the spirit. Do you really think that people pray only when overfed or after excessive drinking, or during the time of careless idleness?

No, men pray in the moments of great difficulty. So too, is this prayer of the spirit most needed when one's whole being is shaken and in want of support, and when it seeks for a wise solution. And wherein lies the stronger support? What will make the spirit shine more brightly?

We do not feel hunger or starvation; we do not shiver because of the cold. We tremble because of the vacillation of our spirit, because of distrust, because of unfounded expectations.

Let us remember how often, when working, we have forgotten about food, and have left unnoticed the wind, the cold, the heat. Our intent spirit wrapped us in an impenetrable veil.

"The weapon divideth it not, the fire bumeth it not, the water corrupteth it not, the wind drieth it not away; for it is indivisible, inconsumable, incorruptible and is not to be dried away; it is eternal, universal, permanent, immovable. . . . Some regard the indwelling spirit as a wonder, while some speak and others hear of it with astonishment, but no one realizes it, although he may have heard it described."–The Bhagavad Gita, Ch. II.

Of what does the great wisdom of all ages and all

nations speak? It speaks of the human spirit. Penetrate in thought into the deep significance of these words and into the meaning of your life. You know not the limits to the power of the spirit. You do not know over what impassable obstacles your spirit bears you, but some day you will awaken, unharmed and everlastingly regenerated. And when life is hard and weary, and there seems to be no way out, do you not feel that some helper, your own divine spirit, is speeding to your aid? But his path is long and your faint-heartedness is swift. Yet does the helper come, bringing you both the 'sword of courage' and the 'smile of daring.' We have heard of a family which in despair put an end to their lives with fumes of charcoal. Now this was intolerably fainthearted. When the coming victory of the spirit arrives, will not they who have fled without orders suffer fearfully because they did not apply their labor as they should have? It matters not what labor. The drowning man fights against the flood by all possible means. And if his spirit is strong, then the strength of his body will increase without measure.

But by what means will you call forth your spirit? By what means will you lay bare that which in man is buried under the fragments of his everyday life? Again and again I repeat: by the beauty of art, by the depth of knowledge. In them and in them alone are contained the victorious invocations of the spirit. And the purified spirit will show you what knowledge is true, what art is real. I am assured that you will be able to call your spirit to your aid. That spirit, your guide, will show you the best paths. It will lead you to joy and victory. But even to victory it will lead you by a lofty path whose steps are bound together by knowledge and beauty alone. . . . An arduous trial awaits the whole world: the trial by assimilation of truth. After the medieval trials by fire, water, and iron, now comes the trial by assimilation of truth. But if the power of the spirit upheld men against fire and iron, then will that same power also raise them up the steps of Knowledge and Beauty. But this test is more severe than the trials of antiquity. Prepare to achieve! Prepare for that achievement which is a matter of daily life. Meanwhile have care for everything that serves to advance the perception of truth. Approach with special gratitude all that shows the stages of beauty. At this time all this is especially difficult.

But adamant-like stand Beauty and Culture—the only road to Peace.

Our motto is: "Humanity is facing the coming events of cosmic greatness. Humanity already realizes that all occurrences are not accidental. The time for the construction of the Culture of the future is at hand. Before our eyes the reassessment of values is being witnessed. Amidst ruins of valueless banknotes, mankind has found the real value of the world's significance. The values of great art are victoriously traversing all storms of earthly commotions. Even the 'earthly' people already understand the vital importance of active beauty. And when we proclaim Love, Beauty and Action, we know verily, that we pronounce the formula of the international language. This formula, which now belongs to the museum and stage must enter everyday life. The sign of Beauty will opens all sacred gates. Beneath the sign of Beauty we walk joyfully. With Beauty we conquer. Through Beauty we pray. In Beauty we are united. And now we affirm these words: 'Not on the snowy heights, but amidst the turmoil of the city and realizing the path of true reality, we greet, with a happy smile, the future.'"

During the days of the present Armageddon I have been asked to send my message to several art exhibitions in India. My message was: Art should be protected by all means. Armageddon is raging. Art and Knowledge are the cornerstones of evolution. Art and science are needed always, but in our days of Armageddon they must be especially guarded by all the powers of our hearts. It is a great mistake to think that during troubled times culture can be disregarded. On the contrary, the need for culture is especially felt in times of war and human misunderstandings. Without Art, Religion is inaccessible, Without Art the spirit of Nationality is lost. Without Art, Science is dark. This is not a utopia. The History of Humanity gives innumerable examples of Art being the great Beacon Light in times of calamity. Scientists assert that color and sound are a panacea. By Beauty and Harmony even wild beasts were tamed. Let the sacred flute of Sri Krishna resound again! Let us visualize that peace in which the majestic frescoes of Ajanta were created! In times of war let us think of future peace affirmed by creativeness, labor and beauty. Traveling through India we passed along a road in the shadow of mighty chinars. Our guide told us: 'The great emperor Akbar thought of the future travelers who were going to be sheltered by these beautiful trees. He looked into the future.' 'To regard the Beautiful means to improve'—said Plato. 'Man becomes that of which he thinks'—preordained the Upanishads.

'A renaissance of art is the evidence of the renaissance of a nation. In a declining country, art becomes only an abstract luxury. But when a country is in its full prowess, art becomes the real motive power of its people. Let us imagine the history of humanity without the treasure of beauty. We will then readily realize that the epochs seem meaningless, stripped of their soul. Without the manifestation of the spirit of the Beautiful, we shall remain amidst the ugliness of death. And when we proclaim that Beauty, Art, is life, we speak about the coming evolution of beauty. Everything accomplished for art is an attainment for evolution. Every coworker in this field is already a hero.

'It is great praise to this country that the list of its creative workers cannot be expressed in one simple list but merits an entire great series of entries, even with the briefest acknowledgments. We are happy to feel what vast material is before us and what a joy it is to show the brilliant legion which has constructed the most beautiful achievements for the young generation. Wherever art and knowledge flourish we may be enthusiasts. And in this joyful enthusiasm we may greet the true creative forces of the nation. An exhibition is not only a monument to the creator, the worker, but it is the best avocation for the youth to come. I am happy to greet the brilliant artists, to hail the essence of beautiful creative thought and to salute the young generation to which this creative thought brings its coming happiness.'

O Bharata, all-beautiful, let me send thee my heartfelt admiration for all the greatness and inspiration which fill thy ancient cities and temples, thy meadows, thy deodars, thy sacred rivers and the Himalayas!

THE ETERNAL GARMENT

MANY years ago, I had a painting, the subject of which was a woman making her first dress. In this painting ornaments were displayed whose design dated from the most ancient times. But the most amazing thing was to see that these ornaments were closely related to the designs which we see today.

You have no doubt also heard of the ancient Scythian art, now in vogue, which is considered the forerunner of Cubism.

In 1922, in Chicago, during the production of the "Snow Maiden", Marshall Field and Company tried to create some modern costumes, employing the styles and ornaments taken from old designs and historic figures. It was really remarkable and very significant to see how some of these models came directly from the most ancient sources of design. It was also astonishing to observe how these historic ornaments had been realized in the most modern way.

In connection with the expression of the old in the new, I am reminded of the time when, in Tibet, I gave some photographs of skyscrapers to the people. They appreciated them most highly because they, in their own country, had skyscrapers since the sixteenth century, in such buildings as the Potala which is seventeen stories high. And not only were these skyscrapers equally high, but one should realize that in the character of their design, they were, in reality, the forerunners of our modern skyscrapers. Thus again, we see that the most ancient and most modern thoughts are being united.

In my Diary, I have found a page dedicated to the production of "Le Sacre du Printemps": "Eighteen years have elapsed since I sat with Stravinsky in the colorful fairy-house, Talashkino in Smolensk, the estate of Princess Tenishev, working on the stage design of "Sacre du Printemps." Princess Tenishev asked us to write some excerpts from 'Sacre' on the beams of this multi-colored house as a memento. Probably some fragments of our inscriptions remain there even now. But who knows if the present inhabitants of this house realize what is written there upon the beams?

"It was a pleasant time when the Temple of the Holy Spirit and my painting, 'Human Forefathers,' were completed. The hills of Smolensk and the white birches, the yellow buttercups and white water-lilies, like the ancient lotuses of India, reminded us of the Shepherd Lei and Koupava or Krishna and the Gopis. In eternal concepts such as these, the wisdom of the East was interwoven with the best images of the West.

"Then war came and I heard that one of my sketches on Stravinsky's estate as well as the sketches of 'Sacre' were destroyed. Many events have occurred but the eternal remains.

"During these years we have witnessed how in all of Asia the eternal rhythm of 'Sacre' resounds in the holy mountains and in the deserts where the songs are presented, not for human beings, but for the great desert itself. When a Mongol refused to repeat his beautiful song to us because 'he sang only for the great desert,' we remembered Stravinsky and how he embodied the eternal rhythm of human striving and the victory of the spirit in the symphony of 'Sacre'. When, in Kashmir, we admired the majestic sight of the festival of Spring with its gorgeous torch dances. I again recalled the powerful musical concepts of Stravinsky.

"When in the mountain monasteries we heard gigantic trumpets and rejoiced before the sacred dances full of rhythmic symbolic movement, again the names of Stravinsky, Stokowski and Prokofiev came to my mind.

"In Sikkim, at the festivals of homage to great Kanchenjunga, we felt the same link with the eternal homage to greatness, which inspired the best poetical images of Siva, who consumed the poison of the world for the sake of Humanity, and of all the great redeemers and heroes, the creators of human ascension.

"During this time, I had already heard that 'Sacre' was acclaimed everywhere and that there no longer exists any conventional prejudice against this expression.

"And I remember how during the first production in Paris, in 1913, the entire audience whistled and roared so that nothing could even be heard. Who knows, perhaps at this very moment they were enjoying themselves, with the same emotions of primitive people. But this savage primitiveness had nothing in common with the refined primitiveness of our ancestors, for whom rhythm, the sacred symbol, and refinement of gesture were great and sacred concepts.

"Well, perhaps it was necessary that thousands of years elapse in order that we might witness how humanity could become conventional and how much prejudice can exist between the listener and the fact. At the same time, it is not so easy to approach the facts honestly. Again, our wretched egoism, conceit and conventionality can hinder and obscure reality. But it is so uplifting to feel that in America, during the ten years of activity, I did not sense any cheap chauvinism or bigotry. Perhaps the new combination of nations preserves America from poisonous pettiness, and the heritage of the great culture of the Mayas and Aztecs gave its heroic background to the great movements of this country. Verily, here in America you do not need to be negative. So many beautiful things are possible if we can keep our positivity and open-mindedness. We can feel how the primal energy is electrified in this country, and this energy provides the easiest way by which you can reach the inner constructive feeling of the nation. This constructive striving of spirit, this joy before the beautiful laws of nature and heroic sacrifices, certainly are the essential feelings of 'Sacre du Printemps.' We cannot consider 'Sacre' as Russian, nor even Slavic. It is more ancient and pan-human.

"This is the natural festival of the soul. This is the joy of love and self-sacrifice, not under the knife of crude conventionality, but in the exuberance of spirit, in connecting our earthly existence with the Supreme.

"Fragments of the 'Sacre' are inscribed on the multi-colored house of the Tenishev estate. Princess Tenishev, the self-sacrificing collector and worker in the field of art has already passed away. Nijinsky is no longer with us, and already Diaghilev rejoices in the higher spheres.

"And still 'Sacre' is new and the young ones are accepting 'Sacre' as a new conception; perhaps the eternal novelty of the 'Sacre' is because Spring is eternal, and love is eternal, and sacrifice is eternal. Thus in this new conception, Stravinsky touches the eternal in music. He was modern because he has evoked the future, it is the great serpent ring touching the great past.

"And the wizard of the Symphony, Stokowski, with his sensitivity for truth and beauty, with his magic, baton, like the eternal priest, again evokes to life the sacred tunes that connect the great past and future.

"The torch festival in Kashmir is so beautiful! So

majestic are the gigantic trumpets in the mountain monasteries! And from beyond Kanchenjunga itself, the great migration with the Eternal Sacre began!"

We know that growth without refinement is undesirable. Everywhere we see expansion without refinement, this growth will express itself in cruelty and rudeness. Another thing which is important: When in 1921, in Arizona, I showed some photographs of the Mongols to some Indians, they said: "Oh, they are Indians! They are our brothers!" And, similarly, when in Mongolia, I showed the Mongols pictures of the American Indians in Santa Fe, they recognized them as their closest relatives. They told me a beautiful fairy tale—how, at one time, there lived two brothers. They told how the earth on which they lived was split, and that since that time these relatives have always been expecting news of one another. They have always been confident that at a certain time they would receive their news. Thus, from the most ancient times, people looked to the future.

When you are in Asia, you see much around you which would be considered as supernatural here. In that country, however, everything is quite natural. We are concerned with the problems which are nearer to life. We dream of having a theater in life. In Asia they have it. During the sacred dances, many sacred designs are seen in Mongolia. Many ancient banners and sacred images are seen in the desert—thousands of people, huge orchestras, beautiful costumes, remarkable designs. Everything there is regarded as an expression of life. If you are allowed to participate in this life you can see no difference between nature and contemporary life; and this is a splendid realization.

In answer to the question as to why they had such tremendously long trumpets with such powerful sound, a lama in Tibet answered that once upon a time a ruler of Tibet wanted to greet a great Teacher from India.

The question arose as to how this Teacher should be greeted. He could not be approached with gold, silver and precious stones. The lama advised the ruler to construct special trumpets, in order to greet the Teacher with new, unprecedented sounds. Again here, the beautiful searching seems so similar to the searching of our days.

Remember the designs of the American Indians in the old pueblos. Before the people were divided into separate nations, they probably had only one language. Thus, in trying to unify the national symbols into one, we can quite easily observe a historic symbol of pure design. The perpetual symbols of nature are collected in this. In the rainbow, lightning, the clouds, we see the history of the striving for the expression of the beautiful—a striving which is the same everywhere, whether we find that expression in Russia, in Mongolia, or in Arizona, it is all the expression of this great human design.

This should be very close to us all because today we are striving toward the next step in evolution. We are trying to discard old forms and create something new. But in order to strive for something new we have first to know the old. Only then can we attain the true enhancement of life.

Now I hear that my friend Leonid Massine, the famous dancer and choreographer is preparing a new staging of the 'Sacre' in the USA. With great difficulties the new sketches were sent from India. Thus during this time of Armageddon, humanity again ponders over Spring, Love and the Beautiful. Let the eternal garment cover the disturbed human mind.

UNITY

"OPEN in all schools the path to creative effort, to the greatness of art. Develop the creative instinct from the earliest years of childhood. Open up the paths of blessing."

The arts are one. What is the creative spirit that abides in all art that is but a breath away from the finer ethers of "worlds before and after?" Music, painting, sculpture, poetry, drama and dance—these are one in essence, one in principle. Do they not spring from the one source—the broadly creative spirit? Are they not all parts of the one life? As petals interwoven and blended, they form the flower of life. They have their home in the timeless and in the endless. That is why a single life is only long enough to catch "hints of the proper craft, tricks of the tool's true play."

To be in harmony with the increasing rate of life's vibration, we find we must make use of the fast-flying wings of the imagination. In our effort to join the worlds within and the worlds without to converge into our "one world," we are re-discovering this principle of unity as it relates to all life. For the basis of true culture, it would seem, lies in the perception, not only of the unity of the arts, but of the unity between art and life. These cannot be dissociated without harm. Where they are severed, life is fragmented and crippled. Seen as one, it becomes an inexhaustible fountain of beauty. When we function truly—with the wisdom of joy—it is with the whole consciousness. In the life of wholeness, as exemplified in the Academy of United Arts, the spirit of each of the arts and of life itself is finely fused and integrated.

Through varying symbols of art, the student sees a world clothed in many veils of beauty. A world "where music, silence and dreaming are one." He learns to seek the goal in creative labor—in striving to become, in the words of Dante, the "Scribe of Eternal Love." Through this service he develops expanded capacities of perception and containment. He finds that the home of the true artist is thus "bounded by the mother-skies;" that "his race is Man; his banner—The Banner of Peace."

When we are concerned with the preservation of cultural values, such excursions through all parts of the state will serve as living custodians of the traditions of Culture. Where instead of destruction born of despair a vibrant home-building is awakened, a garden of beauty also blooms.

What has been said is no abstraction. These affirmations have been tested by many experiences in different parts of the world. Everywhere the human heart remains a true heart and is fed by the beautiful nourishment of Culture.

I recall a beautiful Persian story. Several artisans on a journey had to pass a very wearisome night in a wild locality. But each one had with him his tools and in some ruins a fallen beam was found. And here, during the watch hours, each one of the craftsmen applied his own lofty art to dressing the piece of wood. A wood carver executed the figure of a beautiful girl, a tailor fashioned a garment. Then she was adorned in every way, with the result that a spiritual person with them inspired life in the beautifully created image. As always, the tale ends in full happiness, at the foundation of which lay craftsmanship in various domains.

Another story tells how one of the caliphs, having

been taken captive and wishing to convey news about the place of his imprisonment, wove a rug with conventional signs, as the result of which he was liberated. But for this means of rescue the caliph had to be a skillful weaver.

Yet again I recall a wise covenant of Gamaliel, that declared: "Not having educated his son in arts and crafts, he prepared him for brigandage on the highway." We need not recall the multitude of other highly poetic and practical covenants, but we urgently direct the attention of the schools to such possibilities of highly useful outside work.

Freedom! Freedom! Art as the highest expression of human consciousness must be free to lead Humanity.

THE BEAUTIFUL VICTORY

IN India I was once asked what is the difference between East and West, and I answered: "The best roses of East and West have the same fragrance." So, while we are speaking about opposition and differences, essentially we have the great "One," because really all law is One; and under this law, everything is One. We have only to serve this One; and if we are unable to do so, we may say *mea culpa,* for we are guilty of having failed to follow the law.

Very often we are trying to discover how to build the next life—how to build the next evolution. Well, that is our duty. And all will very soon wish to build up our own lives, and certainly you will wish to build up a happy life. What is the best medium to reach this happiness? Only through the Beautiful. We are divided in so many experiences, and yet everything is this same feeling of the Beautiful. You note that I am underlying the Beautiful, not Beauty, because I am speaking not only about art, or about some expression of art, music, drama, song, but I am speaking about the *sense* of the Beautiful, and it is our duty to introduce into our lives this general sense of this great conception.

Perhaps someone could ask me: "Well, it is very good to have such a dream—to make life somehow beautiful. We often think that this Beautiful is only for those who are rich. And he who must work, how can he dream about the Beautiful?"

In various countries, we have seen many collectors

and real workers in art, and some of them have been very poor. They have been of the working class, and still this sense of the Beautiful was so strong in them that, even with their modest means, they found the possibility to approach the Beautiful.

The chief thing is to have this inner sense of the Beautiful. Because not everyone has the medium in art, but practically everyone has *thought,* and very often our creation in the *realm of thought* is far greater than reflections in some medium of art. I am underlining this because very often people come to me saying over and over the same story: "I have no prospects in life. How can I dream about something beautiful when I have no time to study?" But in a few moments you can see that this man is really gifted—that he has wonderful conceptions and thoughts, and really can project his thoughts and his conceptions into space.

Every thought is recorded in space. So the chief thing is to create in thought—to be real cooperators in this beautiful creation of the whole universe. Because in this way of creation, we will reflect the best creative powers, and then we will really be cooperators and coworkers toward the Supreme.

How can we introduce this spirit here? To do this in a vital way, we have to realize the power of thought. We speak often about willpower, but very seldom do we employ this power. We speak about telepathy, and we think that it is something very difficult and supernatural, phenomenal; but there are no phenomena, and there is no occultism.

To children, even the telephone is a most occult thing. But when you know how energy is employed, you know that there is nothing extraordinary involved.

We should introduce these possibilities into our lives.

In Asia, they speak about *Agni Yoga,* the Teaching of Fire. Is it something supernatural? No. They are explaining how to use this element of Fire—the flame of Space—this all-embracing element. And you will be told that very soon the Era of Flame is approaching our land. You will hear it in a quite scientific way, and then you will remember that Professor Millikan discovered the cosmic ray and is about to discover the keenest application of that ray.

In Asia, for ages and ages, they have spoken about this same beautiful energy. In the Vedas, vital precepts are given.

In the time of the Buddha, they knew about the iron birds that would serve humanity. They knew from the most ancient times about iron serpents, also for the sake of humanity. So, you see how, for ages, real knowledge was being given out but in another language, or with other symbols, for if you will regard our prejudices in full honesty, we can have a multitude of very useful facts.

But the problem is how to approach facts honestly. "We have to take science as science, without any prejudice or superstition." At the same time not infrequently, the scientists themselves fail to regard facts in the pure light of honesty. We should take these facts through ourselves—through our own understanding—and sometimes we will find ourselves more superstitious than some of the people in the desert. When we have such scientists as Einstein, as Millikan, as Raman, we feel that our coming evolution is in good hands.

Is it not a great joy to see how an eminent scientist speaks in so broad a way? In him there is no superstition. And he is experiencing this same state of the Beautiful. Every scientist in the moment of discovery is the same as the artist because he is in the same creative spirit of the Beautiful. Sometime you can ask a discoverer how his discovery was made—what happened in the moment of discovery. And if the man is honest, he will tell you that something happened at that moment. It was not an accident. At that moment, he touched the Supreme—the highest Cross of Eternity.

Some big businessmen are also artists, and it is very easy to speak to and to receive understanding from a big man because his consciousness is already expanded. And if you are speaking to him about something difficult, still his experience is so big that he can understand everything; and from his understanding emanates his tolerance. Please remember this quality—tolerance. You will need it. So many things have been broken through ignorance.

Intolerance is ignorance.

Sometimes we think we are tired. But we are not tired. We are only using the same nervous center too long. If we are tired, it does not mean that we need relaxation—that we need to sleep. We should only change our work—change the center; and in this change of different nervous centers, you will become rested.

Remember, the chief poison is the poison of irritation and anger, and this is a most powerful poison. For, with every irritation, we physically create in our nervous system some poisonous emanation.

Our best scientists and physicians already know that something physical is created through irritation. In Asia, they will tell you about this crystal of anger. How can we be happy if we know that through our anger, we are creating poisons? The only remedy is not to be irritated—not to be angry. When you remember forever that anger is something hideous, then it is not so difficult not to be irritated. If you know that someone is coming to irritate you, you must encounter him with a smile. And when you know that, you are already strong.

I should not like to feel that some of you today think that I am speaking of something abstract, or occult, or something mystical. What is "mystical?"

Something from mist. But we have nothing to do with mists or clouds—only with facts and lights. And with facts we can enlighten our life.

We are speaking about the Beautiful; because when you will realize this scientific energy, the greatest power that is in each of you—then you will release this energy, and energy will grow.

Very often people ask how to release this energy. This energy is our property. One time a young group asked how to release this energy. I asked them: "Each of you, please tell me something unusual about your life." They all became silent. There was nothing unusual to tell! "Our lives are routine." "I am working in a bank." "I am working in a factory." But it is not strange that Boehme, one of the great philosophers, was a shoemaker? And one was a carpenter! Certainly this routine of life is our *pranayama*. That is a new word meaning the use of the energy, the processes of learning how to use the energy. You can achieve through this—but I can tell you that your routine work is the *pranayama*.

When we keep the quality of our work, we begin to be successful. He is the highest artisan, who can attain the quality of art in work. We can even wash the floors spiritually. For then someone will at once remark: "This man is doing this work in such a beautiful way that he is not in his place. Sometimes higher should be given to him." And when we refine the quality of our work, another thing happens—we have the joy of work.

The greatest misfortune is that people often work in expectation of a rest for a holiday; but when we know the joy of work, then we need no conventional holidays. We can celebrate our holiday in labor, with the clearest conception and with the best thought. And we shall not be tired because we shall be enthusiastic, we shall keep our enthusiasm. We shall not sleep too much because we shall not need to sleep much. When we are sleepy, when we are not thinking, then we are not vigilant, and everything bad happens. But if we are producing any work for the quality of the work, in this creative enthusiasm, we are strong and impersonal; this feeling of the impersonal is the greatest aspect of the Beautiful.

Impersonality is the greatest aspect of the Beautiful. Then we can understand that "I" is isolated, and that "We" is strong. Through the "We" is the real beginning of organization, and the real cooperation.

In India we have a beautiful conception of Guruship, the Teacher—it is not a feeling of slavery—on the contrary, it is a great feeling of cooperation. In this way; a chain of cooperators can be created. You know your Master, and someone considers you as a Master; in this way there is a precious chain to the Supreme.

When we know the one Road of Ascent, then many things are easy for us.

CREDO

LYSIPPUS was a blacksmith's apprentice before he ever became a sculptor. The heart of a great artist has never been withered by anguish of a reflective spirit or distress of a hungry body. There is no drought that can destroy the seed of creativeness once it is ready to sprout. Amid the most burdensome labors the folksong sounds a call to renewed creativeness. It is implanted in the quality of each task. Art, knowledge, labor—these are sons of that same creativeness that guides and uplifts.

From the most ancient times, the aims of art have been characterized by the most diverse words. However multiform these definitions may be, everywhere their essence is perceived to be one and the same. First of all from art is demanded persuasiveness. It is said that to be convincing, one must see through beauty. And so it is. To view with the eye of beauty, this means one must comprehend the very best in composition. What sort of composition is this? Much has been said about conventional premeditated arrangement, about a tendency to pretentious subjectiveness. Many times people have tried to express their just indignation at something that in their opinion weighed down the lofty concept of creativeness and rendered it incapable of soaring flight.

Such in reality is conventional composition. In the last analysis artificial composition will always provoke boredom and weariness. But there is also another composition that is natural and yet indefinable in words. The artist may see so clearly and constructively, so to speak, that you do not miss a word of his song. It is precisely as in nature, when the most varied elements are combined in complete harmony. When one examines a cluster of crystals, it is forever amazing how, even when unexpected forms are encountered, they always make up a harmonious, conclusive whole. Thus it is in all artistic creativeness. Its productions have crystallized so naturally that any argument about composition simply falls to the ground. In such a crystal of creativeness is expressed that convincingness that can be definitely felt, but words will be powerless to define it or to give any recipe for it.

When a picture has been naturally built up, you can add or subtract nothing. You cannot shift its parts, and this, not for the reason that you must not violate "symmetry," but that you must not deprive the picture of its vital balance. You have the desire to live with such a picture because you will find in it a constant source of joy. Each object that sheds joy around it represents a veritable treasure. You are indifferent to what school or trend it belongs as an *objet d'art*; it will be a persuasive guide of the Beautiful and will bestow upon you many hours in which you will feel a love for life. You will be grateful to him who has helped you meet life with a smile, and you will take good care of this hieroglyph of Beauty. And you will become better, not at the dry command of morality but from the creative radiation of the heart. In you will awaken the Creator, which is latent in the depths of the consciousness.

In its best disclosures, science proves to be art. Such striking scientific syntheses are forever imprinted upon the human brain as something overwhelmingly conclusive. Then science ceases to be a conventional synchronization of facts and advances triumphantly into the domain of new cognition, leading humanity along with it.

Creativeness, whether it be in symbols or in art, or

in any of the realms ruled by the Muses of the classical world, will be attractive, that is to say, convincing. Science is already entering such immense fields as thought. Now it is coming to light that thought acts according to some sort of laws not set down in human words yet already perceptible in series of experiments being carried on at present. The mind of the thinker will be a creative one.

It has always been required of art that it be creative. This demand is no more than just. After all, art cannot be other than creative. Be it a most intricate picture, landscape, or portrait, once this work emerges from the hands of the true artist, it will be creative. In the complexity of present-day concepts, it may be that the very idea of creativeness has fallen to pieces. Sometimes people begin to assume that creativeness must be expressed in forms having nothing in common with reality. Some may still remember the joke originating at a French exhibition, where a picture turned out to have been painted by a donkey's tail. In their quests of creativeness, instead of liberation (for creativeness must always be free) people begin to seek some new limitation and conventional recipes. In this is forgotten the most fundamental condition of creativeness; first of all, it does not tolerate anything conventionally imposed and self-restrictive.

For example, let us cite Gauguin. Can one possibly call his pictures conventional or tendential? Precisely in the freedom of creativeness, Gauguin strode over all the limiting frames of his subject as well as any sort of restrictive technical rules. He always remains a creative artist, that is to say, a true and convincing master craftsman. The power of persuasiveness of this artist is not in any recipes or rules devised by reason. He has created just as a bird sings, which cannot but sing because its song is the expression of its essential nature. His persuasiveness lies in the fact that he has been capable of viewing each of his pictures as a part of creative nature.

This inner vision of a picture, to the extent that it is requisite and convincing, will always be far outside the methods of technical rules. Creators of all times and peoples have created their productions not only by intuitively seeing them in their best form of expression but by extending their creativeness to the very material in which they worked. The sculptor having inspected the block of marble creates from it the best possible. The master woodcarver employs each quality of his piece of wood in working it into the forms appearing to his creative eye. The painter intuitively selects colorful material for each of his expressions. The artist would probably be unable to explain afterward why precisely he employed oils or tempera or watercolor or pastel. And so it must be. Why does an orator raise and lower his intonation? Why does the musician discover those ineffably enchanting harmonies, which even he cannot always repeat?

Intuition is being much discussed at present. Volumes are being written about intuitive philosophy. The solution of problems is being sought not only in calculations but also in intuitive synthesis. One artist has said: "Do thus, in order that people may believe you." Another, discussing a certain realist, asked: "Does he have to depict all the wayside filth just because it exists in reality?" Yet at the same time let us not condemn realism. Of course, it is only in striving for the actuality that in turn produces that convincingness, for the sake of which one must see with the eye of beauty.

Recently much has been said about the synthesis of art. In all the arts, synthesis is nothing but a condensation of all good possibilities. Once Brulov[*] said, in jest,

---

[*] A famous Russian artist of the mid-nineteenth century.

that art is extraordinarily easy: "One has but to take the right color and apply it in the right place." In essence the master and great technician spoke truly. Precisely one must do what is needful in applying the color, and something whispers what this "needful" is. The master knows when it would be impossible to do otherwise, yet when you ask him by what canons and rules he has done exactly so and not otherwise, no artist can explain to you what laws he followed in doing as he did.

Comparing the works of art of different times and peoples, we see that frequently the most apparently diverse productions go together excellently in a common grouping. One can easily picture to oneself how certain primitives; Persian miniatures; *objets d'art* of Africa, China, and Japan; Gauguin and Van Gogh can all appear in one collection, and even hang on one wall. Not the material or technique but something else enables these entirely different examples to live together in harmony. They are all truly products of creativeness. Moreover, all kinds of art and sculpture, painting, mosaics, ceramics—in a word, absolutely all things in which have been expressed the creative outburst of a master—will be friends and not mutually exclusive antagonists.

Each of us has often listened to contradictory pronouncements. One says that he understands only the old school. Another vehemently raises the objection that all must be in movement and, therefore, he finds joy only in the modernists even though their works may be harsh and strident. Some esteem only oil painting, while others admire the delicate watercolor. Some affirm that they like only "finished pictures," while others assert that they treasure sketches most highly, as the first inspired impulses of the creator. Some can be enraptured only by monumental works, while others feel warm affection for miniatures. Some limit their taste to the grandiose; others find repose of the spirit in small artistic *bibelots.* Do all such limitations denote limitedness of soul on the part of the art lover, or rather, may it not be that these amateurs have simply dammed up their possibilities?

Very often one's preferences and one's collection depend upon some accidental initial impulse. Perhaps some time a man has heard that a picture is painted with oils, and this expression took root in his brain. Perhaps in the family circle a child has been impressed by a word spoken about watercolors, or he may have been given a set of them and from this chance beginning has followed his interest in precisely this medium. In all manifestations of life and particularly in the matter of artistic impulses, one often has occasion to encounter initial fortuity. Indeed, these "accidents" often prove to be for matters of chance. A man has begun to respond precisely to one thing rather than another and, in this, may have been expressed his dormant accumulations. Spring has come, and buds open out naturally, which have long been asleep through the winter cold. New creativeness has begun!

What a beautiful word—"creativeness"! In various languages it rings out appealingly and convincingly. In its own way it speaks about something latently possible, about something triumphant and conclusive. So mighty and beautiful is the word "creativeness" that all conventional obstacles are forgotten in the face of it. People rejoice at this word as a symbol of advancement. The command of creativeness covers over all whisperings of the limited mind about rules, about materials, about all that is so often answered with the suppressive word "impossible." To creativeness, all is possible. It leads humanity along with itself. Creativeness is the banner of youth. Creativeness is progress. Creativeness is mastery of new possibilities. Creativeness is peaceful conquest over stagnation and formlessness. In creativeness has already been implanted movement. Creativeness is the expression of the fundamental laws of the universe. In other words, in creativeness is expressed Beauty.

It has been said that Beauty will save the world. People have smiled at this formula with sympathy or with derogation, but no one can refute it. There are certain axioms that may cause wonder but which one cannot overthrow. Humanity dreams about freedom; it inscribes this great hieroglyph upon the facades of buildings. At the same time, mankind exerts every effort to restrict and reduce this concept. Great freedom of thought is manifested in true creativeness. That will be true that is beautiful and convincing. In the secret places of the heart, for which man himself is responsible, has been implanted trustworthy judgment as to what true conviction is, what creativeness is, what Beauty is.

As Velasquez said: "Not a picture but truth itself."

Let us recall two excellent passages from Anatole France's *Garden of Epicurus.*

"Whatever wins its vogue only by some trick of novelty and whim of aesthetic taste ages quickly. Fashions change in Art as in everything else. There are catchwords that come up, and pretend to be new, just like the gowns from the great dressmakers in the Rue de la Paix; like them, they only last a season. At Rome in the decadent periods of art, the statues of the Empresses showed the hair dressed in the latest mode. Soon these coiffures looked ridiculous, so they had to be changed, and the figures were given marble wigs. It were only fitting that a style as rococo as these figures should be re-periwigged every year. The fact is, in these days when we live so fast, literary schools last but a few years, sometimes but a few months. I know young writers whose style is already two or three generations out of date, and seems quite archaic. This is doubtless the result of the amazing progress of industry and machinery, which sweeps modern communities along. In the days of MM. de Goncourt and railways we could still spend a fairly long time upon a certain form of artistic writing. But since the telephone, literature, which depends upon contemporary manners, renews its formulas with an altogether disconcerting rapidity. So we will merely agree with M. Ludovic Halévy that the simple form is the only one adapted to travel peacefully, not down the centuries, that would be assuming too much but at least down the years.

"The only difficulty is to define what the simple form is, and one must admit this difficulty to be a great one.

"Nature, at any rate as we can know her, and in milieux adapted to life, offers us nothing simple, and art cannot aspire to greater simplicity than nature. Yet we understand well enough what we mean when we say that such and such a style is simple, and such and such another is not.

"I will say this much then, that if there is no simple style, there are styles which appear simple, and it is just these which carry youth and longevity with them. It remains but to inquire whence they get this fortunate appearance. Doubtless we shall conclude that they owe it, not to their being less rich than others in diverse elements, but rather because they form a whole in which all the parts are so well blended that they cannot be distinguished separately. A good style, in fact, is like yonder beam of light which shines in at my window as I write, and which owes its pure brilliancy to the intimate combination of the seven colors of which it is composed. A simple style is like white light. It is complex but does not seem so. This is only a simile after all, and we know what such parallels are worth when it is not a poet who draws them. But what I wished to make plain is this; in language the true simplicity, which is good and desirable, is only apparent, and it results solely from fine co-ordination and sovereign economy of the several parts of the whole."

"If you would taste true art, and experience a profound impression before a picture, examine the frescoes of Ghirlandajo in Santa Maria Novella at Florence, depicting the *Birth of the Virgin.* The old master shows us the room of delivery. Anna, upraised on the bed, is neither young nor beautiful, but one sees immediately that she is a good housewife. She has ranged at the head of the bed a jar of sweetmeats and two pomegranates. A serving-maid, standing between the bed and the wall, offers her an ewer on a platter. The babe has just been washed, and the copper basin still stands in the middle of the floor. Now the infant Mary is taking the breast; her wet-nurse for the nonce is a young and beautiful lady of the city, a mother herself, who has offered her bosom to the end that this child and her own, having imbibed life at the same fount, may keep the savor of it in common, and by force of their blood love each other as brother and sister. Near her stands another young woman, or rather a young girl, like her in features, perhaps her sister, richly dressed, wearing the hair drawn away from her brow, and plaited at the temples like Aemilia Pia; she stretches out her two arms toward the infant with a charming gesture, betraying the awakening of the maternal instinct. Two noble ladies, clad in the Florentine fashion, are coming in to offer their felicitations. They are attended by a serving-maid bearing on her head a basket of water-melons and grapes. This figure is of a large simple beauty; draped in flowing garments confined by a girdle, the ends of which float in the wind, she seems to intervene in this pious domestic scene like a dream of pagan antiquity. Well, in this warm room, in these gentle womanly faces, I see expressed all the life of Florence, and the fine flower of the early Renaissance. This goldsmith's son, this master of the Primitives, has revealed in his painting, which has the clearness and brilliancy of a summer dawn, all the secret of that courtly epoch in which he had the good fortune to live, and which possessed so great a charm of its own that his contemporaries themselves were wont to exclaim: 'The gods are good indeed! Oh, thrice-blessed age!'

"It is the artist's part to love life, and to show us that it is beautiful. Without him, we might well doubt the fact!"

Leonardo ordained:

"He who despises the art of painting, thus despises a philosophic and refined conception of the universe, because the art of painting is the daughter, or rather grandchild of Nature. Everything that exists was born from Nature and has borne, in its turn, the science of painting. This is why I say that painting is the grand-child of Nature and relative of God. He who blasphemes the art of painting, blasphemes Nature.

"The painter must be all-embracing. O artist, may thy multiformity be as infinite as the manifestations of Nature. Continuing what God has commenced, strive to multiply not the deeds of human hands but the eternal creations of God. Never imitate anyone. And every creation of thine, be a new manifestation of Nature!"

History records the manifold remarkable achievements of Leonardo da Vinci in all domains of life. He left amazing mathematical writings; he investigated the nature of flying; he conducted medical researches and was a distinguished anatomist. He invented musical instruments, studied the chemistry of paint; he loved the wonders of natural history. He adorned cities with magnificent buildings, palaces, schools, libraries; he built large military barracks, constructed one of the best ports in the Adriatic, and planned and built great waterways;

he founded mighty forts, constructed war machinery, sketched military plans. . . . Great was his versatility.

But after all these remarkable achievements, he remained in the memory of the world as an artist—as the great artist. Is this not a true victory of Art?

ARMOR OF LIGHT

I REMEMBER how Puvis de Chavannes always found a sincere, benevolent word for the most different creations. But I cannot forget how another famous artist used to go around all exhibitions but with the foam of bitter criticism that he defamed. I noticed that he spent about three-quarters of an hour on abuse and only a quarter of an hour on rejoicing. Taking leave of the artist, I said, "I know how to make you stay longer—with things that are detestable to you!" And the abuse of this artist was most refined, but his praise very poor and dry. Of course, in his creativeness Puvis de Chavannes was far higher. Did not the benevolent criticism of Puvis originate because of his greater creative ability?

Why disparage and act maliciously where a general enthusiasm and a general joy of creativeness have been ordained?

Since time immemorial innumerable are the commandments about the beautiful. Whole kingdoms, whole civilizations were built by this great ordainment. To beautify, to ennoble, to uplift life means to reside in the good. All understanding and all forgiveness and love and self-denial are generated in the attainment of creativeness.

And should not all young hearts strive for creativeness? And so they do; and plenty of ashes of vulgarity are required to choke this sacred flame! How often can one open new gates to the beautiful by the single call,

"Create, create"! How much decrepitude is expressed in the fossilized program: First, I shall learn to draw; then, I shall go over to colors; and after this, I shall try to start composition. Innumerable are the cases when the flame of the heart was extinguished before the pupil reached the forbidden gates of creativeness! But how much joy, daring, and vigilance is developed in the consciousness of those who from their childhood dared to create! How enticingly attractive can children's composition be before their eyes and hearts become hardened by the all-deadening conditions of standard!

Where are the conditions of creativeness? In the genius, in the imperative tremor of the heart, which calls forth constructiveness. The earthly conditions are of no importance for the creator who has been called. Neither time, nor place, nor material can limit this impulse of creativeness. "Even if imprisoned, an artist will become an artist," was one of the sayings of my teacher, Kuindzhi. But he also used to say, "If you have to be kept under a glass cover, then the sooner you disappear the better! Life has no need for such touch-me-nots." He understood well the significance of the battle of life, the battle of light and darkness. A small clerk came to the teacher; the latter praised his work, but the clerk complained: "Family and office stand in the way of my work."

"How many hours do you spend in the office?" asked the artist.

"From ten to five."

"And what are you doing from four to ten?"

"What do you mean, from four to ten?"

"Yes, from four in the morning?"

"But I sleep."

"Well, then you will spend your whole life sleeping. When I worked as a retoucher with a photographer, our work was from ten to six; but the whole morning from four to nine, I had at my own disposal. And to become an artist, even four hours per day are sufficient."

Thus said the venerable master Kuindzhi, who, beginning as a shepherd boy, through labor and unfolding of his talent reached an honorable place in the art of Russia. Not harshness but knowledge of the laws of life suggested to him his replies, full of realization of his responsibility, full of consciousness of labor and creativeness.

The main thing is to avoid everything abstract. It does not exist in the actuality just as emptiness does not exist. Every recollection of Kuindzhi, of his teachership, both in the art of painting and in the art of life, always brings to memory unforgettable details. How necessary are these milestones of experience when they bear witness of tested valor and of actual constructiveness!

I remember, how after my graduation at the Imperial Academy of Arts, the Imperial Society for the Encouragement of the Arts invited me to become assistant editor of their periodical. My colleagues were indignant at such a combination of activities, and prophesied the end of my art. But Kuindzhi firmly advised me to accept the appointment, saying: "A busy person succeeds in everything. An open eye perceives everything. But for a blind man to paint is anyhow impossible." I remember how Kuindzhi once criticized my painting *The March*. But half an hour later he returned short of breath, having run up to the studio, and said smilingly, "You must not be grieved. The ways of art are innumerable. The main thing is that the song comes right from the heart."

Another teacher of mine, Puvis de Chavannes, who was full of well-wishing and inexhaustible creativeness, always called with profound wisdom for the labor, self-expression, and joy of the heart. Love for humanity and the joy of creativeness were not dead in him, but one will remember that his first steps were not encouraged.

For eleven years his paintings were not accepted by the Salon. This was a hard testing-stone for the greatness of the heart!

My third teacher, Cormon, always encouraged me to individual, independent work, saying: "We become artists when we remain alone by ourselves.'

Blessed are the teachers when they lead with a benevolent, experienced hand toward wide horizons. It is a great happiness when one can remember one's teachers with the full tremor of a loving heart.

The teachership of old India, the deep conception of Guru—teacher—is especially touching and inspiring. Yes, it is inspiring to see how a free, conscious veneration for the teacher existed until today. Verily, it forms one of the basic beauties of India. No doubt the same conception existed also among the old masters of Italy, and the Netherlands, and among Russian icon painters. But in these countries it is already a beauty of the past; whereas in India, it is living and will not die out, I hope.

Every spiritual impoverishment is shameful. From the subtler worlds the great masters are watching sorrowfully, grieving over the folly of impeded possibilities. In the articles *"Spiritual Values," "Revaluation,"* and *"Flame—the Transmuter,"* we spoke sufficiently about everything that should not be lost at the crossroads. I cannot forget the deep saying of my deceased friend, the poet Alexander Block, about the ineffable. Block ceased to frequent the Religious Philosophical Society because, as he expressed himself, "They speak there of the unspeakable." Precisely, there is a limit to words; but there is no limit to feelings, to the capacity of the heart. Everywhere is the beautiful. All pilgrims of the good, all sincere searchers landed at this coast. People may quarrel ever so much and may even become like beasts, but still they will unitedly be silenced at the sound of a mighty symphony and will desist from all quarrels in a museum or under the dome of the Notre-Dame in Paris.

The same love of the heart is evoked when we read in all ordainments the lightnings of beauty.

The Persian apocrypha about Christ is most touching: "When Christ was walking along with his disciples, they came across the carcass of a dead dog, lying near the roadside. The disciples turned away in disgust from the decaying corpse. But the teacher found beauty in this instance and pointed out the beautiful white teeth of the dog."

At the hour of passing, Buddha the Lord remembered: "How beautiful is Rajagriha and the cliff of the vulture! Beautiful are the valleys and the mountains. Vaishali! What a beauty!"

Every Bodhisattva, besides all his other abilities, has to also be perfect in art.

The Rabbi Gamaliel says: "The study of the law is a noble work if connected with some art. This occupation, which is accompanied by art, leads away from sin. But every occupation that is not accompanied by art leads nowhere." And the Rabbi Jehuda adds, "He who does not teach his son art, makes of him a highway robber." Spinoza, who reached considerable perfection in art, answered indeed to this ordainment of harmonization and ennoblement of the spirit.

Of course, the high ordainments of India also affirm the same basic significance of creative art. "In ancient India, art, religion, science were synonymous with Vidya, viz., culture." "*Satyam, Shivam, Sundaram* are the eternally triune manifestation of godhood in man—immutable, blissful, and beautiful."

Let us remember the Museion—the home of the Muses—of Pythagoras, Plato, and all those great ones who understood the cornerstones of the foundations of life, and Plotinus—speaking on the beautiful!

From the depths of hard experiences of life, Dostoevsky exclaims, "Beauty will save the world!" Ruskin, who glorifies the stones of the past, reiterates the same. A well-known head of the church looking at paintings, exclaimed, "A prayer of earth to Heaven!"

The old friend of all creative searchers, Leonardo da Vinci, says:

"He who despises the art of painting, thus despises a philosophic and refined conception of the universe, because the art of painting is the daughter, or rather grandchild of Nature. Everything that exists was born from Nature and has borne, in its turn, the science of painting. This is why I say that painting is the grandchild of Nature and relative of God. He who blasphemes the art of painting, blasphemes Nature.

"The painter must be all-embracing. O artist, may thy multiformity be as infinite as the manifestations of Nature. Continuing what God has commenced, strive to multiply not the deeds of human hands but the eternal creations of God. Never imitate anyone. And every creation of thine, be a new manifestation of Nature!"

The "stubborn sternness" of Leonardo da Vinci—was it not strengthened by the clear joy for the far-off worlds, by the firm prayer of the heart for Infinity?

How many of the best personalities affirmed the prayer of the heart, the prayer for beauty, for the beauty of creativeness, for victories of Light! From all lands in all ages, many affirm the significance of creativeness as the leading principle of life. Ancient monuments retain glorious images of Egypt, India, Assyria, Maya, and China; and are not the treasures of Greece, Italy, France, Belgium, and Germany living witnesses of the significance of highest creativeness?

How wonderful that, even now, amid all spiritual and material crises, we can affirm the kingdom of the beautiful! And we can do this, not as abstract idealists but armed with the experience of life and strengthened by all historical examples and spiritual ordainments.

Remembering the significance of creativeness, humanity must also remember the language of the heart. Are not the parables of Solomon, the Psalms, the Bhagavad Gita, and all fiery commandments of the hermits of Sinai written in this language? How precious it is to realize that all ordainments lead not to division, this limitation, and not to savagery but to the ascent, the strengthening, and purification of the spirit!

Dr. Brinton reminded me that when leaving America in 1930, I told him, "Beware of the barbarians." Since then many barbarians have broken into the domain of culture. Under the sign of financial depression many irremediable crimes have been committed within the wall of the spirit. The list of dark oppressors, like tablets of shame, has indelibly been recorded on charts of education and enlightenment. Uncultured retrogrades hastened to destroy and uproot much in the field of education, science, and art! Shame, shame! Chicago has no funds to pay the municipal teachers. A church in New York has been sold in auction. In Kansas City, the capitol has been sold in the same way. And how many museums and schools have been closed! And how many hardworking men of science and art have been thrown overboard! Yet the horse races were visited by fifty thousand people! Shame, shame! The stones of ancient monuments can cry out against all the apostates of culture, the source of everything blissful and precious. Do not the scorners of culture trample their own well-being? Even the blind ones see more than these gloomy servants of darkness.

"Beware of the barbarians!"

Still, we cannot be reconciled with an unstable value. We can unite only on the steps of culture, in the name of everything, creative, beautiful. Still it will always be considered a good and noble deed to support everything creative and educational. Ascending these steps, we ourselves become enlightened.

Assembling around the sign of culture, let us remember how we addressed womanhood: "When there are difficulties in the home, we turn to the woman. When accounts and calculations are no longer of aid, when enmity and mutual destruction reach their limits, we turn to the woman. When evil forces overcome one, the woman is invoked. When the statistical mind becomes helpless, then one remembers the woman's heart."

And thus now, times are difficult for the universal abode of culture. And again we hope that the heart of the woman will understand the grief for hampered creativeness, for culture. She will understand the grief for spiritual treasures and will come to aid in realms of the beautiful.

Youth should not be educated upon the wails of despair. When we wrote about the preordained beautiful gardens, we did not lure into illusory domains. On the contrary, we called to the strongholds, affirmed by life. Especially in the days of distress we must affirm the prayer of the heart to the beautiful. We must remember that the beautiful is within the reach of everyone.

To rise from a shepherd boy to venerated masterhood, like Kuindzhi, or for a remote peasant to become a beacon of science, like Lomonosov, is certainly not easy. Seemingly nothing helped them. Everything was as if against them, and yet "Light conquers darkness!"

As children we liked the book *Martyrs of Science.* It is really necessary that there also should be published books on *Martyrs of the Spirit, Martyrs of Art, Martyrs of Creativeness.* The life dramas of Van Gogh, Gauguin, Rider, Vrubel, Mares, and many martyrs for the beautiful make one more unforgettable ordainment that leads the youth. "Gratitude is the virtue of great hearts." Let us not only remember the glorious names with gratitude, but let us arm ourselves with the whole of their experiences in order to confront all destructive forces of darkness. The experience of creativeness forges all those invincible "Armor of Light" of which the apostle speaks. Now is an urgent hour, when one must be armed with all the experience of the past in order not to surrender the stronghold of culture. Now is the time to be aware of the whole spiritual treasure of creativeness in order to repel with this "Armor of Light" the dark forces of ignorance and to move onward fearlessly! *Per aspera ad astra!*

It is not joyful that we can, notwithstanding varied parties, address every sincere artistic group with the hearty greetings: "Despite all kinds of disunity, the human spirit turns again to positive constructiveness, when every sincere cooperation is appreciated. Do not many kinds of different flowers grow upon the spring meadows, and are they not magnificent in their diversity? Does not this creative multiformity manifest in its fragrance the festival of the spring, which is celebrated by all people since time immemorial?"

Nothing can replace the divine multiformity. So also in the earthly reflection of Divinity in art, multiformity means bountifulness of the people's spirit. Amid the disasters of humanity, we feel more the value of creativeness.

May constructiveness and the beautiful desire for the good—in other words, that which is to be laid at the foundation of all activities of a cultural man—resound. Everywhere man feels oppressed under conventional divisions, terrible in their insignificance; he is suffocated by the stench of ignorance, by the poison of non-culturedness, which poisons all existence.

All to whom human dignity is dear, all who strive toward truly preordained perfection must naturally work together, casting off, as shameful rags, the dictionary of malice and lies, remembering that in the dictionary of good, there are many non-abstract really vitally applicable conceptions. And now, undeferrably, these conceptions must be applied in life so that the word ceases being an empty sound but becomes the actual strengthening factor of creative thought.

Everyone striving toward the good knows how valuable are all the so-called obstacles, which for a virile spirit are only measures of strength, and which in their tension work out but a new and transmuted energy.

It is not yesterday that is being affirmed. One can affirm but the tangibility of the future. As long as we shall not be convinced in our hearts of the radiant constructiveness of the future, we shall remain in hazy abstraction. For the future trees are being planted along the roadside, and for the future the milestones are being erected. The builder would not put up milestones if in his heart he could not know whither this path leads.

We affirm—this path leads to knowledge, to the beautiful; but this knowledge will be freed from all prejudices and will follow the aims of the good. We affirm—this road leads to beauty, and not luxury or caprice; but everyday's necessity will impel the striving and realization of the beautiful on all paths. We shall not be afraid of the conception of reality. Those who strive in valor know all conditions of the path.

As the wise ones say: "Before leaving, one does not pronounce unkind words." The weak ones will say, "The heart became weary. But what lives in infinite love, leading toward realization in discipline of the spirit and in beauty, will not become weary and overfilled." By tension and burdening of the heart, we increase our experience. Let us be guided by the beautiful words of the wisdom of the East:

Tire Me now, load Me better, laying upon Me the burden of the world.

But I will multiply the strength.

Dost thou hear? The load will blossom with roses and, the grass will be garbed in the rainbow of the morning.

Therefore tire Me.

When I am nearing the garden of beauty, I do not fear burden.

In wisdom everything is real, and the morning is real and the beautiful garden is real; and the burden and the weariness of the world and transfigured attainment are also real.

THE HOUR

Awaken, O friend. A message has come.
Ended, thy rest.
Now I have learned where is guarded
One of the Sacred Signs.
Think of the joy if
One sign we shall find
Before sunrise we shall have to go.
At night we must all prepare.
Look at the night-sky. . . .
It is beautiful as never before;
I do not remember
Such another.
Only yesterday
Cassiopeia was sad and misty,
Aldebaran twinkled fearfully
And Venus did not appear.
And now they are all ablaze.
Orion and Arcturus are shining.
Far behind Altair
New starry signs

Are gleaming and the mistiness
Of the constellations is clear and transparent.

Dost thou not see
The path to that
Which tomorrow we shall find?
The starry masses have awakened.
Take thy fortune.
The armor we shall not need.
The shoes put tightly on,
Tightly girdle thyself,
Our path will be stony.
The East is aflame.
For us
    Is the hour.

CREATORS

BY the sign of beauty, the locked gates may be opened. With song, one can approach a wild yak so that she loses her fierceness and submits to milking. With a song one may tame horses. Even the serpents hearken to a song. It is significant to observe how healing and exalting is the touch of beauty.

Often we have had occasion to write of the importance of the so-called applied arts. Many times we compared the so-called higher arts with no less significant manifestations of all the branches of artistic industry. It is even dreadful to have to repeat again that the "button" created by Benvenuto Cellini is not only not inferior to but undoubtedly far superior to multitudes of average paintings and graveyard sculpture. These comparisons are old; and it would seem that reminders are no longer necessary, but life itself indicates quite the opposite.

In all fields of life, the sphere of applied art, which is blatantly stamped with some such shameful appellation as "commercial art," is abruptly separated from the general understanding of art. Instead of a gradual realization of the unity of the substance of creation, humanity seems to be striving to divide itself still more pettily, and to spread mutual humiliations. It would also seem absolutely apparent that the style of life is created not merely by great individual creators but by the entire body of artists in the applied arts. It is not always their hands that create a poster or a work of jewelry. By some inexplicable curiosity, the products of ceramics are considered inferior to sculpture in marble, although the charm of the Tanagra has given us ample evidence of a noble folk creation.

One may still hear the sorrowful exclamation of many young people: "I cannot live by art. I have to enter the commercial field," thus implying that by this act, the artist dooms himself to the inevitable disgrace that is presumed to accompany participation in practical art.

What material, what circumstances, could deprive an artist of his quality? What manner of demand would compel him to do anything artistic in any expression of life? What type of promoter would destroy the creative fire which gushes unrestrainedly through all materials? It is important for each promoter, even for the most elementary and inartistic one, that his product be clear, vivid and convincing, and easily assimilated by the masses in their daily life. After all, which of these conditions may be regarded as disgraceful? Raphael himself, after receiving his order, was guided by the condition of conviction. Truly the quality of conviction in no way contradicts the true artistry.

Gauguin, through sheer desire for self-expression, painted the doors and interior of his dwelling in Tahiti. Vrubel placed his "Swan Princess" on a platter. The number of examples is countless, in which the most diverse artists sought for expression through the most extraordinary materials. As we have previously noted, the material itself, by its very subtle quality, lends a special conviction to the object. Is there any need to repeat the identical examples that have been mentioned as often in widely varying circumstances? Not discussion but action should strengthen the attitude so necessary for culture. If we reach the expression of the unity of arts, we thereby affirm the need of the closest correlation of all branches of art in its various materials.

It would be difficult to indicate a defined order in

which such workshops could be conducted side by side with sketching, drawing, and life classes. This order must be left to life itself. In each country, in each city, and even more, in each district of the city, there are special impressions of life. Hence to these problems one must respond to first. Near a large textile factory, it would be good to provide drawing and study of the technique of this industry. Near ceramic and porcelain factories, one could lend assistance precisely to this medium—thus expanding and refining the understanding that one should correlate in the immediate neighborhood, the practical expressions prompted by the closest possibility. Incidentally, one should not overlook the fact that the physical environment of three of these workshops will afford reciprocal assistance and provide unsuspected combinations that will afford new and fascinating possibilities. The open mind of an instructor, unhampered by prejudice, and the broad demand for creativeness from the students will result in that living vibration that, uncongealed by monotony, will afford to the craft shops an endless, practical variety and conviction.

Another gracious quality is gained through the manifestations of practical variety. They temper the spirit, freeing it from the sense of limitation, which so often constructs our dwelling of fear. But it is from fear, above all, that each aspect of creation must be liberated. In fear, creation cannot be free; it will bind itself with every chain, and forget the noble and victorious discipline of the spirit. Long ago it was said: "One must be cured of fear." One must pursue such methods consciously to liberate oneself from that fear of dusky pettiness and the creeping phantoms that caused even the stone that fell from heaven, aflame with a heavenly fire, to become opaque. Truly, opaque and veiled, when it could have been transparent for all, this Scarab of light!

The Egyptians called artists and sculptors *seankh* or "revivifiers, resurrectors." In this definition is manifested a deep comprehension of the substance of art. How immeasurably broadened this concept can become if we apply it to all manifestations of life, when we acknowledge that each adorner of daily life is an "artist of life." And this true "revivifier" of everyday life himself will be uplifted with new power, will become imbued with the creative spirit in ennobling each object of daily life. Then the shameful and hideous understanding of "commercial art" will be cast out of usage. We shall call this noble adorner of life an "artist of life." He must know life; he must feel the laws of proportions. He is the creator of the needed forms, the evaluator of life's rhythms. To him, numbers, correlations are not dead signs but the formulas of existence.

Pythagoras calculates and creates, sings praises in rhythms, prays in rhythm because numbers were not only the earthly but the heavenly rhythms—the music of the spheres. With Pythagoras, the mathematician, resounds also St. Augustine, the theologian: *Pulchra numero placent.* "Beauty enchants by number." This magnet of number proportions, correlations, and technical consonances, necessary for each of life's adorners, precludes all diminishing of disintegration of the great creative understanding.

Do not let us fear to speak in the highest terms of each manifestation of beauty. A solicitous, exalted expression is a shield for all practical art, which is often exiled to the obscurity of the cellars. A country that is mindful of the future should protect all—from the smallest to the greatest—for whose vindication it will be responsible at the great Judgment of Culture. Facilitating the destiny of these builders of life, the country of culture only fulfills the fundamental covenant of the Beautiful, so beautifully expressed by the poets of antiquity: *Os homine sublime dedit coelumque tueri.* "I gave to man a lofty forehead that he should perceive the summit."

With an exalted covenant the Bhagavad Gita confirms the multiformity of creation: "By whatever path you come to Me, by that path shall I bless thee."